WALK 1 > QUIRINAL HILL, TREVI FOUNTAIN & PANTHEON p. 18

The Quirinale is one of the seven hills. Look out over the entire city from the presidential palace, throw a coin into the Trevi Fountain, and have a coffee near the Pantheon.

WALK 2 > VILLA BORGHESE, SPAGNA & PIAZZA DEL POPOLO p. 38

In the Villa Borghese park you'll find a zoo and an open-air theater. Go window shopping near the Spanish Steps.

WALK 3 > VATICAN, PRATI & PIAZZA NAVONA p. 58

The Vatican is fascinating. Climb up to the basilica's dome or walk through Prati, an upscale neighborhood. Street artists on Piazza Navona create a magical vibe.

WALK 4 > CAMPO DE' FIORI, GHETTO & TRASTEVERE p. 78

Campo de' Fiori is always alive and bustling, partly thanks to the morning market. Taste traditional dishes in the Jewish neighborhood and enjoy the vibrant Trastevere's restaurants and delightful bars.

WALK 5 > TERMINI, MONTI & FORI IMPERIALI p. 98

Relive ancient times in the various museums. Hip wine bars make the Monti neighborhood very attractive, and the Imperial Forum and Colosseum capture the imagination.

WALK 6 > ROMA... TESTACCIO p. 118

Walk along the once-bustl... ...entino Hill to the workers' distric... ...rom the busy tourist center.

D1410484

1

ROME WALKS

Step off the plane and head straight for the newest, hippest coffee joint in town. Discover where to get the best seafood in the city or where to find locally brewed beer on tap. In *Moon Rome Walks*, our local authors let you in on all the hotspots and best kept secrets. This way, you can skip the busy shopping streets and stroll through the city at your own pace, taking in a local attraction on your way to the latest and greatest concept stores. Savor every second and make your city trip a truly feel-good experience.

ROME-BOUND!

You're about to discover Rome. According to legend, Rome was built in 753 B.C., and almost 2,800 year later, the city has developed a modern vibe. Ancient theaters found new life as restaurants, and workers' districts are now hip yuppie neighborhoods. The Colosseum, the Foro Romano, the Vatican, and the Spanish Steps—these are just a few of the monuments that support Rome's status as "the Eternal City." Every street corner provides an opportunity to explore something from a different era, and in between all that history is the here and now: strong Italian coffee, ice cream in all imaginable flavors, wine from Rome's region of Lazio, pasta a-la-Romana, and hidden independent businesses. Follow us and we'll unveil all the secrets of the Eternal City!

ABOUT THIS BOOK

In this book, local authors share with you the genuine highlights of their city. Discover the city by foot and at your own pace, so you can relax and experience the local lifestyle without having to do a lot of preparation beforehand. That means more time for you—what we call "time to momo." Our walks take you past our favorite restaurants, cafés, museums, galleries, shops, and other notable attractions—places we ourselves like to go.

None of the places mentioned here have paid to appear in either the text or the photos, and all text has been written by an independent editorial staff. This is true for the places in this book as well as for the information in the **time to momo app** and all the latest tips, themed routes, neighborhood information, blogs, and the selection of the best hotels on **www.timetomomo.com.**

CITY
ROME

WORK & ACTIVITIES
TEACHER

LOCAL
TESSA D.M. VRIJMOED

Tessa always looks farther than the general tourist attractions. From the quiet courtyard of the Chiostro del Bramante, to the Testaccio neighborhood where you can eat with the locals at Pizzeria Nuovo Mondo, she will make you fall in love with the magic of this city, especially with its beautiful museums and plentiful concerts.

PRACTICAL INFORMATION

The six walks in this book allow you to discover the best neighborhoods in the city by foot and at your own pace. The walks will take you past museums and notable attractions, but, more importantly, they'll show you where to go for good food and drinks, shopping, entertainment, and an overall fun time. Check out the map at the front of this book to see which areas of the city the walks will take you through.

Each route is clearly indicated on a detailed map at the beginning of the relevant chapter. The map also specifies where each listing is located. The color of the number tells you what type of venue it is (see the key at the bottom of this page). A description of each place is given later in the chapter.

Without taking into consideration extended stops at various locations, each walk will take a maximum of three hours. The approximate distance is indicated at the top of the page, before the directions.

PRICE INDICATION
We give an idea of how much you can expect to spend at each location, along with its address and contact details. Unless otherwise stated, the amount given in restaurant listings is the average price of a main course. For sights and attractions, we indicate the cost of a regular full-price ticket.

WHEN IN ROME
Your idea of efficiency will probably be challenged when visiting Rome. So, relax and don't worry too much when you can't find an up-to-date timetable, if a res-

---

LEGEND

● >> SIGHTS & ATTRACTIONS   ● >> FOOD & DRINK
● >> SHOPPING   ● >> MORE TO EXPLORE

taurant opens later than their sign says, or when a museum closes sooner than listed.

Eating is a vital part of Italian life. Romans tend to eat late. Lunch is usually from 1pm to 3pm, and only the most touristy restaurants open their doors before 8pm for dinner. Avoid restaurants where waiters stand outside praising the menu. Instead, visit a Roman *trattoria, osteria,* or family restaurant with no pretense. Romans are not good with change, but slowly and steadily more trendy restaurants and bars are opening their doors. At these trendy places, it's more about seeing and being seen than the quality of the food. For truly good food, choose basic places with fluorescent lights and paper table covers. An *enoteca* is a wine bar where you can enjoy small bites and light fair, while in a *ristorante* you'll sit down to an elaborate meal—often chic and with service some other places lack. On the bill you'll generally see a cover charge of two to three euros per person, listed as *coperto* or *pane*. If you see this charge listed, don't tip unless the service was exceptionally good. If there is no cover charge on the bill, a 10% tip is customary.

The Roman kitchen is famous for its simple dishes, such as *pasta alla gricia* (with pork jowl) or *cacio e pepe* (with cheese and black pepper), fried specialties like stuffed zucchini flowers or *baccalà* (salted cod), and hearty meats like lamb shank or oxtail. Italians like to drink wine with their meals and usually start with an *aperitivo* with a few small bites. After a hearty meal, they order a *digestif:* a distilled drink like *grappa* or *limoncello* that "massages" the insides.

Romans don't have elaborate breakfasts. They tend to have a cappuccino and a *cornetto* (croissant) at their neighborhood bar. Pay at the checkout first, then take your receipt to the bar to collect your order. Within two minutes you're out. You can be served at a table, but you will be charged slightly more.

GOOD TO KNOW
Most shops close for lunch—roughly between 1:30pm and 3pm—and they remain closed all day Sunday and Monday mornings. Many shops and restaurants close for the entire month of August. This is less common in the city center, but don't be surprised at how quiet it can be in other neighborhoods. Museums often close their cash registers an hour before the official closing time. Are you under 18 or a student under 26? Take your passport or student card with you when you visit a museum. You'll get a discount but only upon identification.

If you want to visit churches, keep a modest dress code in mind. Bring a light scarf to cover your shoulders on warm summer days, and make sure that bare legs are covered. Skirts or shorts that fall below the knees are often okay.

MUSEUM REVOLUTION
Italian museums instated a new policy in July 2014. Museum tickets used to be free for seniors 65 and older, but now they have to pay full price. Only kids 18 and younger and (in some cases) teachers have free entrance. Students under 26 get a discount.

As compensation, "museum nights" are organized twice a year, which feature a €1 entrance fee. Major attractions like the Colosseum remain open until 10pm every Friday night. And all museums are free the first Sunday of every month.

This policy change was decided by Minister Dario Franceschini of the "Ministero dei Beni e delle Attività Culturali e del Turismo" (Ministry of Cultural Heritage and Activities and Tourism) to honor the value of Italian heritage. Before this change, more than one in three visitors had free admission to museums, which made the Minister feel like he was "sitting on a gold mine."

PUBLIC HOLIDAYS

August is the main holiday month in Italy, so keep in mind that many shops and restaurants in Rome are closed for vacation *(chiuso per ferie)*. Italy also recognizes the following public holidays:

January 1 > New Year's Day
January 6 > Epiphany *(La Befana)*
April 25 > Liberation Day
May 1 > Labor Day
June 2 > Republic Day
August 15 > Assumption of Mary *(Ferragosto)*
November 1 > All Saints' Day
December 8 > Immaculate Conception
December 25 > Christmas Day
December 26 > St. Stephen's Day *(Santo Stefano)*

HAVE ANY TIPS?

Shops and restaurants in Rome come and go fairly regularly. We do our best to keep the walks and contact details as up to date as possible, and this is reflected in our digital products. We also do our best to update the print edition as often as we can. However, if, despite our best efforts, there is a place that you can't find or if you have any other comments or tips about this book, please let us know. Email info@momedia.nl, or leave a message on **www.timetomomo.com.**

TRANSPORTATION

A taxi from **Leonardo da Vinci-Fiumicino Airport** to the center of town is €48, and €30 from Ciampino Airport. Note: This rate is only available within the historic

center. Many unofficial taxi drivers try to scam tourists at both airports, so only get into a white cab with a taxi meter. You can also take a **shuttle bus** to central Termini station *(www.sitbusshuttle.it, www.terravision.eu)*. The **train** is also an option: One way on the Leonardo Express train from Fiumicino to Termini costs €14, and a train to Trastevere station is €8.

Rome has three subway lines. A and B pass by all the major sights and cross each other at Termini station. Line C is still partly under construction, so expect regular changes to the schedule. Normally the **subway** runs from 5:30am until

11:30pm (Fri & Sat until 1:30am). The **bus** takes you to all the places the subway doesn't, but they can be jam-packed and a favorite spot for pickpockets. With the subway and buses #40 and #64, you can cover most of the center. Tickets for the subway, bus, **tram,** and train are €1.50 and valid for 100 minutes. Stamp your ticket when you board. Note: You can use one ticket to transfer subway lines, but you have to stay within the entry gates. Tickets are sold at tobacco shops and subway stations. You can choose from 1-day tickets (€7), 2-day tickets (€12.50), 3-day tickets (€18), and 1-week tickets (€24). Night buses run between midnight and 5am. More info is available at: *www.atac.roma.it.*

A Roma Pass is valid for 3 days. You can use it for public transport and it grants free access to two museums. The pass costs €36 and is sold at various tourist information booths, all participating museums, and a few subway stations. More info is available at: *www.romapass.it.*

Taxis are not allowed to stop on the street and can only pick up customers at taxi stops. Make sure your driver resets the meter. Luggage comes with a surcharge. Rides after 10 pm, on Sundays, and on national holidays start from €5. You do not have to tip. You can also order a **taxi** by calling (0039) 06 3570.

While Rome's center is small enough to explore on foot, the adventurous may be interested in renting a **motor scooter** (about €40/day). You need a driver's license and must wear a helmet. Rental scooters are available at Treno & Scooter on Piazza del Cinquecento, in front of Termini station *(www.trenoescooter.com).* Be careful—traffic is chaotic.

BIKING

Don't be surprised if you find a bike path that stops suddenly: this is an example of vain attempts to make the city more bike-friendly. The rows of holes, which until recently held poles with rental bikes, are silent witness to this, too.

Yet, in recent years more cyclists have started to take to the city streets. Rome is built on several hills, so not every neighborhood is easily accessible by *bici.*

A number of highlights in the historic center, however, are on flat terrain, including the neighborhoods around the Vatican, Piazza Navona, Pantheon, Piazza del Popolo, Trevi Fountain, Campo de' Fiori, and the ghetto.

There are relatively few bike paths in Rome, especially in the center. Visit *www.piste-ciclabili.com* to study an overview of all the bike lanes (green lines). Want to go for a proper bike ride in the heart of the city without constantly having to navigate the busy traffic? Go down to the riverside and ride the *lungotevere*— a long path running along the riverbank. Be vigilant elsewhere in the city. The average Roman driver is not very attentive of people on bikes. And if your bell doesn't work, shout *"Attenzione!"* ("Watch out!"). There are two golden rules in Roman traffic: Wear a helmet, and don't be in a hurry.

Topbike Rental & Tours in Via Labicana 49 is an organization of enthusiastic people who love to show off Rome and its rich history by bike. Have a look on their website or call for more information *(www.topbikerental.com,* t 064882893). Alternative options include Bici & Baci *(www.bicibaci.com)* and Roma Rent Bike *(www.romarentbike.com).*

Bici Roma *(www.biciroma.it)* is one of the organizations that wants to push the political agenda for more new bike lanes. A large bike tour is held annually throughout the city in collaboration with the Dutch embassy in Rome.

Italy is one of the top five countries in the world with the most cars. Wouldn't it be wonderful to avoid the headache of navigating by car and instead chain your bike to a drainpipe in front of the Pantheon?

TOP 10 | RESTAURANTS

1 Go to **L'Arcangelo** for a creative dinner in the chic Prati neighborhood. > p. 70

2 Lunch with the locals in **Hostaria Romana.** > p. 29

3 There are endless choices at **Roscioli.** > p. 90

4 **L'Asino d'Oro**'s lunch menu is excellent. > p. 113

5 Always a cozy feel in the long and narrow **Cul de Sac.** > p. 70

6 Every day features a different dish at **Felice a Testaccio.** > p. 133

7 Vegetarian food in the modern **Il Margutta Ristor Arte.** > p. 53

8 **Grappolo d'Oro Zampanò** is an innovative trattoria. > p. 89

9 For kosher food go to **Ba'ghetto.** > p. 90

10 **Taverna Pretoriana** is always buzzing. > p. 109

TOP 10 | FILM LOCATIONS

1 **Cinecittà** is a world-famous film set. > p. 141

2 Anita Ekberg bathes in **Fontana di Trevi** in *La Dolce Vita*. > p. 25

3 Legendary **La Bocca della Verità** in *Roman Holiday*. > p. 129

4 In *Quo Vadis*, Petrus sees Jesus on **Via Appia Antica.** > p.139

5 Tom Hanks looks for *Angels & Demons* on **Piazza del Popolo.** > p. 46

6 Statues from the **Vatican** in *The Godfather Part III.* > p. 58

7 *The Talented Mr. Ripley* goes to **Piazza di Spagna.** > p. 45

8 *La Grande Bellezza* opens at **La Fontana dell'Acqua Paola.** > Via Garibaldi

9 **Trastevere** is the backdrop of *To Rome With Love*. > p. 78

10 **Porta Portese** plays a part in *Bicycle Thieves*. > p. 141

1 See the pope after Sunday mass at **Piazza San Pietro.** > p. 62

2 **Palatino** and **Foro Romano** form the heart of old Rome. > p. 122

3 Relive ancient times with a walk through **Ostia Antica.** > p. 139

4 View the impressive Etruscan art collection at **Villa Giulia.** > p. 42

5 Brunch is served after you see the exhibition in the **Chiostro del Bramante.** > p. 71

6 Romans love to swim in **Lago di Bracciano.** > p. 142

7 Many great finds at the **Porta Portese** Sunday market. > p. 141

8 Summertime operas in **Terme di Caracalla.** > p. 141

9 Climb up to the **Vittoriano** and enjoy the view. > p. 117

10 **Open Baladin** proves that beer is increasingly popular in Italy. > p. 90

TOP 10 — NIGHTLIFE

1 **The Auditorium** is the cultural center of Rome. > Viale Pietro de Coubertin 30

2 Bustling **Ponte Milvio** in North Rome. > Piazzale di Ponte Milvio

3 Sip summertime cocktails on the **Isola Tiberina.** > Isola Tiberina

4 See the **Minerva Roof Garden views. >** Piazza della Minerva 69

5 Go clubbing in **Testaccio.** > Via di Monte Testaccio

6 **Cohouse Pigneto** suprises with a new chef every three weeks. > Via Casilina Vecchia 96

7 The young and trendy **Pigneto neighborhood.** > Via del Pigneto

8 **Byron** is a cozy bar. > Via Ostiense 73

9 Go clubbing at **Vinile restaurant.** > Via Giuseppe Libetta 19

10 Classics in the **Globe Theatre Roma.** > Largo Aqua Felix

WALK 1

QUIRINAL HILL, TREVI FOUNTAIN & PANTHEON

ABOUT THE WALK

This scenic walk will lead you past some of the city's most important sights, as well as plenty of shops and typical Roman restaurants. To get a taste of real Roman city life, don't stick to the route religiously. Instead, do as the Romans do, and roam around, stopping for a chat here and there with some of the local shopkeepers and artisans. This is also a perfect route to follow by bike.

THE NEIGHBORHOODS

Rome is the heart of the Roman Empire, the seat of the Catholic Church, and the capital of Italy. The city's diversity manifests itself in churches, palaces, and museums at every turn.

Quirinal Hill is one of the Seven Hills of Rome. At its top lies the **Piazza del Quirinale,** with its enormous presidential palace majestically overlooking the city. **Fontana di Trevi** is an impressive fountain, and legend has it that when you toss a coin in the water over your left shoulder using your right hand, you will return to Rome. It's usually a bit quieter at night, when the fountain is beautifully lit.

You'll find shopping arcade **Galleria Alberto Sordi** on Piazza Colonna, a favorite for shoppers and Art Nouveau aficionados alike. And be sure to admire the impressive art collections on display at nearby **Palazzo Doria Pamphilj,** which is privately owned by the princely Roman Doria Pamphilj family, who still lives here.

The area surrounding the **Pantheon,** one of the best-preserved monuments from ancient times, is buzzing with little shops and Roman *trattorias*. These time-honored eateries have been around for decades. Waiters dressed in black and white serve up classic dishes like *pasta all'amatriciana*. This is also a great place to stop for coffee, with two of the oldest and most famous coffee bars in town.

WALK 1 DESCRIPTION (approx. 3.4 miles)

Start at the crypt on Via Veneto ❶. Admire Triton ❷ on Piazza Barberini and check out the movie schedule ❸. Take Via delle Quattro Fontane. Turn right onto Via degli Avignonesi if you're in need of a massage ❹ and turn left onto Via del Boccaccio for a Roman lunch ❺. Take Via Rasella to go back to Via delle Quattro Fontane. Farther down you will see Palazzo Barberini ❻ on your left. Keep walking until you reach the fountains ❼, then turn right. You will soon reach Sant'Andrea al Quirinale ❽. In need of a coffee? Palombini Espozioni ❾ requires a small detour, but you can stop for lunch nearby ❿. If you're looking for some shade, head to the gardens ⓫. View the presidential palace ⓬ from Piazza del Quirinale, then head down the steps next to it. Take Via della Dataria and visit an archaeological site ⓭. For ice cream, turn right onto Vicolo dei Modelli ⓮. Walk back and head toward the Trevi Fountain ⓯. For shopping, walk through Via delle Muratte ⓰ and turn right onto Via di Santa Maria to get to the Galleria Alberto Sordi ⓱. Via del Corso is also great for shopping. The Column of Marcus Aurelius ⓲ stands tall on the square across the street. Walk through Via dei Bergamaschi until Piazza di Pietra, where you can have lunch with a view of the stock market ⓳ ⓴. Take Via de Burrò and view the Sant'Ignazio di Loyola church ㉑. At the end of Via di Sant'Ignazio, cross the parking lot to visit a museum ㉒, or have a drink around the corner. Turn right onto Via di Piè di Marmo for chocolate ㉓ and jewelry ㉔. Continue walking for wine with a view ㉕ to Piazza della Minerva ㉖. Bear left behind the Pantheon for stationary ㉗. Have a slice of pizza ㉘ or delicious fresh coffee at Sant'Eustachio ㉙. To see some art by Caravaggio, head right down Via della Dogana Vecchia until you reach the French church ㉚. Via Santa Giovanni d'Arco, farther ahead on the left, takes you to Ai Monasteri ㉛. Take the first right, onto Via di Sant'Agostino, and order a steak at Via delle Coppelle ㉜. Explore the many boutiques in this neighborhood, such as L'Autre Chose ㉝. Choose Via degli Uffici del Vicario for artisan gelato ㉞, or head south on Vicolo della Guardiola for coffee ㉟. Marvel at the sudden appearance of the majestic Pantheon ㊱. Enjoy a great meal ㊲ and let all the impressions of the day sink in.

SIGHTS & ATTRACTIONS

①The **Santa Maria della Concezione** hides a gloomy scene: The bones of 4,000 monks decorate the five chapels in the crypt. Some are fashioned into Christian symbols, but you will also see full skeletons wrapped in habits. There's a message for visitors in the last chapel: "What you are now, we once were; what we are now, you shall become."

via vittorio veneto 27, www.cappuccinivineveneto.it, t: 0688803695, open daily 9am-6:30pm, entrance €8, metro barberini

②In the middle of Piazza Barberini, you'll find **Fontana del Tritone** (Triton Fountain). It was designed in 1642 by sculptor Gian Lorenzo Bernini and features four dolphins holding up a seashell, upon which a muscular Triton kneels. The fountain base features a depiction of bees—a symbol of the powerful Barberini family.

piazza barberini, metro barberini

⑥The impressive **Palazzo Barberini** was built in the 18th century for the powerful Barberini family. Inside, the door on the right leads you up a spiral staircase by architect Francesco Borromini. The wide, monumental staircase behind the door on the left was designed by his rival, Bernini. This staircase takes you to the **Galleria Nazionale d'Arte Antica,** with paintings from the 16th and 17th centuries, including a portrait of Raphael's alleged lover, *La Fornarina* (the baker's daughter). Also visit the Galleria Corsini. The tour through its private family rooms with frescoes in the Sala delle Battaglie is a definite highlight.

via delle quattro fontane 13, www.galleriaborghese.it, t: 0632810, open tue-sun 8:30am-7pm, entrance €7, metro barberini

⑦On the highest point of the street lie the **Quattro Fontane**—four fountains that represent the Tiber and Arno rivers and the goddesses Diana and Juno. This is also where the **San Carlo alle Quattro Fontane** church is located—Borromini's first solo project. This church epitomizes the Baroque style, and Borromini used optical tricks to make it look like the dome is floating.

via delle quattro fontane, www.sancarlino.eu, t: 064883261, open mon-fri 10am-1pm & 3pm-6pm (summer only in the morning), sat 10am-1pm, sun noon-1pm, free entrance, metro barberini

⑧ Bernini had limited space for the **Sant'Andrea al Quirinale.** He designed this oval church in 1658 and made it appear quite spacious because of the deep chapels. This charming little Baroque gem is a popular location for weddings.
via del quirinale 29, www.gesuitialquirinale.it, t: 064874565, open tue-sat 8:30am-noon & 2:30pm-6pm, sun 9am-noon & 3pm-6pm, free entrance, metro barberini

⑫ The **Piazza del Quirinale** offers a fantastic view of Rome and the dome of St. Peter's Basilica. At 200 feet, the Quirinale is the highest of the seven hills. The fountain on the square displays a mixture of old Roman statues, an Egyptian obelisk, and a water bowl from the Middle Ages similar to an animal trough. The enormous **Palazzo del Quirinale** was built in the 16th century as a summer house for the pope. For a long time it served as the royal palace, and since 1947 it has been the official residence of the president of the Italian Republic. The palace looks rather plain from the outside, but its luxurious halls are staggeringly beautiful. One of the halls has the same structure and dimensions as the Sistine Chapel in the Vatican.
piazza del quirinale, www.quirinale.it, t: 0639967557, open tue-wed & fri-sun 9:30am-4pm (reservations required, see website), closed aug, entrance €5, metro barberini

⑬ The **Insula del Vicus Caprarius** is an archaeological site exhibiting the underground relics of an ancient apartment building *(insula)* where poorer Romans used to live. It also shows how this building was transformed into a luxury house *(domus)* for the wealthier classes, and eventually became a water reservoir.
vicolo del puttarello 25, www.romasotterranea.it, t: 3397786192, open wed-fri 11am-5:30pm, sat-sun 11am-7pm, price €3, metro barberini

⑮ Anita Ekberg's midnight swim in the **Trevi Fountain** is world famous, but don't try to imitate this scene from the movie *La Dolce Vita*—the ornately decorated Rococo fountain is very well guarded. Between the goddess of abundance (on the left) and the goddess of health (on the right) stands Neptune. The water flows through an aqueduct dating back to ancient times. Toss a coin into the fountain with your right hand over your left shoulder—legend has it that doing this guarantees that you will return to Rome one day. The money goes to charity and amounts to roughly €950,000 per year.
piazza fontana di trevi, bus fontana di trevi/metro barberini

⑱ Standing almost 100 feet tall, the **Column of Marcus Aurelius** is located in the middle of the Piazza Colonna. The picture relief winding around the column reads like a comic book, telling the story of wars waged by this Roman emperor in the 2nd century. Piazza Colonna is the center of political power in Italy, where you'll find Palazzo Chigi, the official residence of the Italian Prime Minister.
piazza colonna, bus piazza san silvestro

㉑ The **Sant'Ignazio di Loyola** church was built at the end of the 17th century. It is dedicated to Ignatius of Loyola, founding father of the Society of Jesus (Jesuit order). Because the Jesuits decorated the interior with an abundance of frescoes, gold leaf, and marble, they didn't have any money left to construct a dome. Andrea Pozzo solved this problem by painting a striking illusion of a dome.
piazza di sant'ignazio 8, www.chiesasantignazio.it, t: 066794406, open mon-sat 7:30am-7pm, sun 9am-7pm, free entrance, bus largo di torre argentina

㉒ Since the 17th century, the spacious **Palazzo Doria Pamphilj** has been home to the descendants of this wealthy aristocratic family. Inside is the **Galleria Doria Pamphilj,** with one of the most prominent art collections in Italy, including paintings by Velázquez, Caravaggio, Titian, and more. The audio tour features the voice of a living family member—a prince, no less. You can also visit the **Caffè Doria,** a beautiful café with an authentic indoor fountain.
via del corso 305, www.doriapamphilj.it, t: 066797323, palazzo open daily 9am-7pm, café mon-sat 7:30am-8pm, sun 10am-6pm, museum entrance €12, wine bar €6, bus piazza venezia

㉖ Piazza della Minerva features a large marble elephant with an obelisk on its back, designed by Bernini. In the original Gothic church **Basilica di Santa Maria sopra Minerva,** you'll find Michelangelo's statue of Christ the Redeemer. The body of the patron saint of Italy, Catharina of Siena, is buried beneath the altar. Her head, however, is located in the church of her hometown Siena. In the monastery next to the church, Galileo Galilei was interrogated by the Inquisition until he finally relinquished his belief in the Copernican model of the solar system.
piazza della minerva 42, www.basilicaminerva.it, t: 0669920384, open mon-fri 7:30am-7pm, sat 7:30am-12:30pm & 3:30pm-7pm, sun 8am-12:30pm & 3:30pm-7pm, free entrance, bus/tram largo di torre argentina

Basilica di Santa Maria ad Martyres

㉚ **San Luigi dei Francesi** is a French church in Rome. The church is famous mostly for its three Caravaggio paintings in the fifth side chapel on the left, depicting the life of Matthew.

piazza san luigi dei francesi 5, www.saintlouis-rome.net, t: 06688271, open mon-wed & fri-sun 10am-12:30pm & 3pm-6:45pm, thu 10am-12:30pm, free entrance, bus corso del rinascimento

㊱ Everything about the **Pantheon** is impressive. It was built from A.D. 118 to 128, after a fire destroyed the first building from A.D. 27. The "temple for all gods" was converted to a church in the 7th century. Its perfectly circular dome symbolizes the heavens above. This was the first ceiling made of cement and, 2,000 years later, it is still intact. The walls supporting the dome are 21 feet thick. The only natural light source is the open oculus in the ceiling. An original Roman drainage system was built into the colored marble floor. Artist Raphael preferred to be buried here rather than in St. Peter's Basilica. You will also find the royal Italian tombs here.

piazza della rotonda, www.pantheonroma.com, t: 3478205204, open mon-sat 8:30am-7:30pm, sun 9am-6pm, holidays 9am-1pm, free entrance, bus largo di torre argentina

FOOD & DRINK

⑤ **Hostaria Romana** has been a genuine classic among Roman *trattorias* for over 50 years now. This is a bright space with a pleasant feel, where the waiters still wear black and white. It's perfect for a quick lunch with the locals. Order the *bucatini all'amatriciana* (pasta with pork jowls and pecorino cheese) or *spaghetti alla carbonara*.

via del boccaccio 1, www.hostariaromana.it, t: 064745284, open mon-sat 12:30pm-3pm & 7:15-11pm, price pasta €13, metro barberini

⑨ Caffetteria **Palombini Esposizioni** is located inside the Palazzo delle Esposizioni, the largest exhibition area in the city. The café sits next to a bookstore and is somewhat hidden inside the building. It has a white, minimalistic interior and a menu featuring sandwiches and savory snacks, like cold pasta and grilled peppers. The courtyard is lovely, as well. Open Colonna, the fancy restaurant in the Palazzo, is also worth a visit.

via milano 15-17, www.palazzoesposizioni.it, t: 0648941320, open tue-fri & sun noon-8pm, sat noon-11pm, price sandwich €5, bus via nazionale

⑩ **LasaGnaM,** a fast-food restaurant specializing in lasagna, was founded by four successful poker players. Their lasagnas are all prepared with fresh and locally-sourced ingredients. Try the Genovese or the Calabrese with handmade meatballs. They also have fantastic baked goods. This is a great option if you're in the mood for a quick and authentic Italian lunch.

via nazionale 184, www.lasagnam.it, t: 0648913677, open mon-thu 7:30am-10pm, fri 7:30am-11pm, sat 10am-11:30pm, sun 10am-10pm, price lasagna €6.50, bus via nazionale

⑭ **Il Gelato di San Crispino** sells top-quality ice cream, offering some 20 seasonal flavors, such as wild orange. Compared to other places, where gelato generally consists of nothing but artificial flavorings and colorings, San Crispino has remained immensely popular despite the fierce competition.

via della panetteria 42, www.ilgelatodisancrispino.it, t: 066793924, open sun-thu noon-12:30am, fri-sat noon-1:30am, price ice cream from €2.70, bus fontana di trevi

⑯ For good food in a non-Italian setting, go to **Baccano.** This restaurant and wine bar feels like an early-20th-century Parisian bistro, complete with cozy seating, dark wood panels, and mirrors on which the menu is written. The food, however, is proper Italian: They make traditional dishes with top-quality ingredients.

via delle muratte 23, www.baccanoroma.com, t: 0669941166, open daily 10am-2am, price €20, metro barberini/bus fontana di trevi

⑲ You'll find several places for lunch on Piazza di Pietra, across from the Temple of Hadrian (now the stock market). **Osteria dell'Ingegno** (*"osteria* of the mind") is a smart option. It's a bright and cheerful restaurant serving salads and other dishes that are a tad more original and substantial than elsewhere. This is a great option for an aperitif or dinner.

piazza di pietra 45, t: 066780662, open daily noon-midnight, price salad €12, tram piazza venezia

㉑ **Salotto 42** sells design books you can thumb through, as well as a carefully chosen selection of CDs. It's a popular spot for a tea or coffee break, or lunch at the raw-food buffet. At night it transforms into a chic cocktail lounge.

piazza di pietra 42, www.salotto42.it, t: 066785804, open daily 10am-8pm, lunch buffet 12:40pm-3pm, aperitif 7pm-10pm, brunch sat-sun 1pm-4pm, price lunch buffet €12, aperitif €10, brunch €20, bus largo di torre argentina

㉕ The panoramic view of the Pantheon from the luxurious **Minerva Roof Garden** at the Grand Hotel de la Minerve is simply superb. Choose from over 300 wines, or try oysters and champagne.

piazza della minerva 69, www.minervaroofgarden.it, t: 06695201, open daily 12:30pm-3pm & 7:30pm-11pm, price wine €12, bus/tram largo di torre argentina

㉘ Grab a slice of pizza at **Zazà,** where they use organic ingredients. Try toppings like truffle and ricotta cheese or chicory and brie. They only have outdoor seating.

piazza di sant'eustachio 49, www.pizzazaza.it, t: 0668801357, open mon-sat 9am-11pm, sun 9am-midnight, price pizza slice from €2, bus largo di torre argentina

㉙ Follow the scent of fresh coffee and you'll find **Sant'Eustachio il Caffè.** According to many Romans this is the best coffee house in town, rivaled only by Tazza d'Oro. Sant'Eustachio il Caffè opened its doors in 1938 and roasts its beans on the premises in wood-fired ovens. The coffee comes sweetened, so ask for a *"non zuccherato"* if you don't want sugar. The deer in their logo, also visible on the eponymous church on this square, alludes to the conversion of St. Eustace.

piazza di sant'eustachio 82, www.santeustachioilcaffe.it, t: 0668802048, open sun-thu 8:30am-1am, fri 8:30am-1:30am, sat 8:30am-2am, price caffè zuccherato €1.20, bus largo di torre argentina

㉜ **Maxelâ** (Genoese for "butcher") distinguishes itself from other shops by selling classic Roman dishes as well as outstanding meat. The unique decor includes window sills covered with corks and glasses constructed from empty wine bottles.

via delle coppelle 10-13, www.maxela.it, t: 0668210313, open mon-sat 12:30pm-3pm & 7:30pm-11pm, price pasta €10, bus corso del rinascimento

㉞ People have been flocking to **Giolitti** for good artisan gelato since 1900. This chic ice salon is always extremely busy. Line up at the register first, then stand in line again to order from the many delicious flavors. If you want to sit, you'll pay for table service, but the ice cream is just as tasty standing up!

via degli uffici del vicario 40, www.giolitti.it, t: 066991243, open daily 7am-1pm, price ice cream €2.50, bus via del corso

㉟ Rivaling Sant'Eustachio, **Tazza d'Oro** is a serious contender for the best coffee in Rome. Tazza also roasts and grinds its coffee on the premises. Take home a few bags, although you may struggle to replicate the wonderfully creamy layer on your espresso at home. In the summer you can order a *granita:* incredibly strong coffee with freshly whipped cream.

via degli orfani 84, www.tazzadorocoffeeshop.com, t: 066789792, open mon-sat 7am-8pm, sun 10:30am-7:30 pm, price coffee €0.90, bus largo di torre argentina

㊲ Cork wall tiles, a stained-glass door, and a menu that has remained the same for decades, **Armando al Pantheon** is an institution for old-school Roman dining at its best. The menu features many classic dishes with organ meats, as well as specialties such as chickpea pasta and guinea fowl with porcini mushrooms. Reservations are recommended.

salita dei crescenzi 31, www.armandoalpantheon.it, t: 0668803034, open mon-fri noon-3pm & 7pm-11pm, sat noon-3pm, price pasta €12, bus largo di torre argentina

SHOPPING

㉓ **Moriondo e Gariglio** has warm red walls and so many ribbons it'll feel like you're inside a box of chocolates. This chocolate shop was opened in 1886 by two master chocolatiers from Turin, the chocolate capital of Italy. Besides bonbons, they also sell beautiful marzipan and candied fruits.

via del pie'di marmo 21-22, t: 066990856, open mon-sat 9am-7:30pm, bus largo di torre argentina

㉔ An elegant piece of jewelry doesn't necessarily need to be crafted from gold or silver. Glass, ceramics, papier-mâché, or aluminum can work just as well. **Materie** sells very unique jewelry, as well as scarves and bags made from silk and velvet.

via del gesù 73, www.materieshop.com, t: 066793199, open mon-sat 10:30am-7:30pm, bus largo di torre argentina

㉗ Just one visit to **Cartoleria Pantheon dal 1910** will inspire you to put all your impressions of Rome down on paper. This amazing little shop has everything you could possibly need for writing, from stationary to pens, beautiful albums, fun stamps, and stylish bags. This shop has been in business for over a century.

via della rotonda 15, www.pantheon-roma.it, t: 066875313, open daily, winter 10:30am-7:30pm, summer 10:30am-8pm, bus/tram largo di torre argentina

㉛ For centuries monks have been using plants and herbs to make salves, brew drinks, and create other concoctions. At **Ai Monasteri** you'll find the best products from monasteries throughout Italy, such as honey and *grappa*.

corso del rinascimento 72, www.aimonasteri.it, t: 0668802783, open mon-sat 10:30am-7:30pm, closed thu afternoon, bus corso del rinascimento

㉝ **L'Autre Chose**'s brightly lit, large window displays offer a good sampling of the romantic dresses and high heels you can purchase here. This is where modern women go shopping for contemporary business fashion.

piazza campo marzio 9-11, www.boccaccini.it, t: 066878542, open mon 3pm-7pm, tue-fri 10am-7pm, sat 10am-7:30pm, bus corso del rinascimento

MORE TO EXPLORE

③ Need to take a break from all the hustle and bustle? Then head to **Multisala Barberini** and get lost in the magic of the silver screen. Slowly but surely more and more theaters in Rome are beginning to screen movies in their original language (not dubbed), and this is one of them. This is a rare find in Italy, so make sure to book your ticket in advance.

piazza barberini 24-26, www.cinemadiroma.it, t: 0686391361, open mon-fri 3pm-1am, sat-sun 11am-1am, price €8.50, metro barberini

④ Being a tourist in Rome can be physically demanding—you can unwittingly end up covering long distances. The masseuses at **Kami Spa** will get to grips with your achy feet and muscles. As soon as you leave the Roman traffic jams behind you, you will begin to feel zen again. Choose from Asian massages, body packs, scrubs, and other spa treatments. There is also a lovely swimming pool.

via degli avignonesi 12, www.kamispa.com, t: 0642010039, open daily 10am-10pm, see website for prices, metro barberini

⑪ The small, shady gardens along **Via del Quirinale** offer a welcome retreat on a hot, sunny day. The 16th-century **Giardini del Quirinale,** however, are only open on June 2nd—*Festa della Repubblica,* or Republic Day, a public holiday.

via del quirinale, www.quirinale.it, open daily from sunrise to sunset, free entrance, metro barberini

⑰ Shopping mall **Galleria Alberto Sordi** has been open since 1922, but was only recently renamed for the famous Italian actor. The gallery is built in Art Nouveau style, with archways and high stained-glass ceilings. Take a break and have a coffee in the central café.

via del corso, tegenover piazza colonna, www.galleriaalbertosordi.it, t: 0669190769, open mon-fri 8:30am-9pm, sat 8:30am-10pm, sun 9:30am-9pm, bus piazza san silvestro

WALK 2

VILLA BORGHESE, SPAGNA & PIAZZA DEL POPOLO

ABOUT THE WALK

This considerably long walk features plenty of shopping and a laidback visit to the park. The park is also easily accessible by bike, which will leave you more time. The second part of this walk, which focuses on shopping, can be shortened by visiting only the stores that interest you—and there is a shop for every taste.

THE NEIGHBORHOODS

The park at **Villa Borghese** was created over 100 years ago, and for many Romans, this is the only garden they have. Here they enjoy romantic evening strolls together, or go for walks with the entire family. The park is full of wonderful attractions, such as the world's smallest cinema and a zoo. There are also plenty of cultural sights, such as the **Galleria Borghese,** which houses one of the most impressive art collections in the world, and the **Villa Giulia** museum, with its impressive collection of Etruscan art and artifacts.

The Pincian Hill looks out over the **Spanish Steps** above **Piazza di Spagna.** The steps are great for people watching: Italian playboys and foreign handbag vendors offer up a free daily show—there's never a dull moment.

For fashionistas with exorbitant tastes and equally sizable expense accounts, this neighborhood is heaven on earth: Gucci, Prada, Armani, and every other noteworthy Italian fashion designer can be found here. And for mere mortals, window shopping offers plenty of fun too. Those on a more conservative budget can still indulge in some of the more affordable shops in this neighborhood, especially on **Via del Corso,** one of Rome's major shopping streets.

Pastificio serves pasta for just a few euros, and the tiramisu at **Bar Pompi** is the stuff legends are made of. **Via Margutta** used to be home to many artists, and

SIGHTS & ATTRACTIONS

③ **Galleria Borghese** is home to one of the most important art collections in the world. Camillo Borghese sold over 500 artworks to his brother-in-law Napoleon to settle his enormous debts. Those works are now on display at the Louvre in Paris, but the pieces that stayed in Rome are unparalleled, and include works by Raphael, Caravaggio, Rubens, and Titian. See how legends are brought to life in Bernini's sculptures *Apollo & Daphne* and *The Rape of Proserpina*. The semi-nude Venus statue of Paolina Borghese (Napoleon's sister) by Canova made her husband very jealous indeed.

piazzale del museo borghese, www.galleriaborghese.it, t: 0632810, ticket counter open tue-sun 8:30am-7:30pm, entry times 9am, 11am, 1pm, 3pm, 5pm (reservations mandatory), entrance €11, metro flaminio/bus viale san paolo del brasile

⑥ The **Galleria Nazionale d'Arte Moderna e Contemporanea** (GNAM) houses the national collection of 19th- and 20th-century art and is located in an ornately decorated building. It features the work of most contemporary Italian artists, including the Futurists. These artists from the beginning of the 20th century were inspired by industrialization and technological progress.

via delle belle arti 131, www.gnam.beniculturali.it, t: 0668802323, open tue-sat 8:30am-7:30pm, sun 2pm-7:30pm, entrance €8, metro flaminio/bus piazza thorwaldsen

⑦ The **Museo Nazionale Etrusco di Villa Giulia** is housed in a Renaissance palace that was once Pope Julius III's summer residence. The Etruscan civilization dates back to before the Romans. The Etruscans had a written language and were skilled artisans, as can be seen from the hundreds of tools on display at the museum. They had a huge influence on Roman culture. Highlights of the museum include the terracotta *Sarcophagus of the Spouses*, from around 530 B.C., and a collection of ceramics decorated in red and black.

piazzale di villa giulia 9, www.villagiulia.beniculturali.it, t: 063226571, open tue-sun 8:30am-7:30pm, entrance €8, metro flaminio/bus piazza thorwaldsen

⑪ The **Trinità dei Monti** church was founded in the early 16th century and commissioned by Louis XII. Giacomo Della Porta, Carlo Maderno, and Domenico Fontana played important roles in the completion of the church. These three

this quiet street still breathes an atmosphere of creativity. Wander from gallery to gallery to get a sense of its unique vibe.

This part of the city is also home to many bars and restaurants. Some of them are world-famous, while others are hidden gems. There are also some important sights to see, such as the **Ara Pacis** altar—dedicated to Pax, the Roman goddess of peace—and the obelisk at **Piazza del Popolo.**

SHORT ON TIME? HERE ARE THE HIGHLIGHTS
+ VILLA & GALLERIA BORGHESE + PIAZZA DI SPAGNA + ARA PACIS
+ PIAZZA DEL POPOLO + VIA MARGUTTA

TIPS

// Recommended for travelers with children
// Note limited opening hours at most shops on Sundays
// Reverse this route and finish with a picnic in the park

CCIXI

men also helped build St. Peter's Basilica. Note the frescoes from 1541 by Daniela da Volterra, including the famous scene of the descent from the cross. The obelisk in front of the church dates back to Imperial times and is a Roman copy of many Egyptian examples. It likely decorated the race track in the imperial gardens.

piazza della trinità dei monti 3, www.trinitadeimonti.net, t: 066794179, open tue-sun 6:30am-8pm & thu until midnight, free entrance, metro spagna

⑫ Take a seat on the Spanish Steps and watch the countless bag salesmen and tourists taking pictures. A total of 138 steps connect the Trinità dei Monti church to the rest of the city. They offer a view of **Piazza di Spagna,** named after the 17th-century Palazzo di Spagna, home to the Spanish embassy.

piazza di spagna, metro spagna

⑬ When Pietro Bernini, the father of the famous Gian Lorenzo, was asked to design a fountain for the foot of the Spanish Steps, he was faced with quite a challenge: The pressure in the aqueduct at that particular spot was very low. He came up with an ingenious solution by creating a partially sunken boat *(barcaccia)*. Gian Lorenzo completed the **Fontana della Barcaccia** after his father's death in 1629.

piazza di spagna, metro spagna

⑮ The 17th-century **Sant'Andrea delle Fratte** church is dedicated to the holy Andreas. The angels at the sanctuary were originally designed by Bernini to decorate the Ponte Sant'Angelo, where replicas stand today. Around the corner, at #12 on Via della Mercede, you'll find a plaque commemorating Bernini's house—although he actually lived at #11.

via di sant'andrea delle fratte 1, www.santandreadellefratte.it, t: 066793191, open daily 6:15am-1pm & 4pm-7pm, free entrance, metro spagna

㉔ Augustus was Rome's first emperor and heir to Julius Caesar. The **Mausoleo di Augusto** was designed as a monumental mausoleum for his family and himself. But throughout history, the building has been used and abused in many different ways. It served as a fortress during the 12th century, and was a concert hall from 1908. Mussolini's fascists wanted to revive ancient Rome, and dug up the tomb and surrounding area in 1936. The white angular buildings around the square also stem from this time.

piazza augusto imperatore, www.sovraintendenzaroma.it, t: 0667103238, temporarily closed for restoration, metro spagna/flaminio

(25) The modern building surrounding the **Ara Pacis** (Altar of Peace) was the first new construction to go up in the city center since Mussolini's time. However, its controversial design—by American architect Richard Meier—is often referred to as a cesspit. The altar itself was built between the years 9 and 19 B.C. in honor of the stability brought back to the Roman world by Emperor Augustus. The marble reliefs depict figures who helped lay the foundations of Rome and a procession of the imperial family. After the Roman Empire fell, the altar was looted. Many years later, after countless excavations and years of international negotiations, the pieces were completed again and Mussolini had the altar restored to its original state.

lungotevere in augusta/corner via tomacelli, www.arapacis.it, t: 060608, open daily 9:30am-7:30pm, entrance €10.50, metro spagna/flaminio

(34) **Piazza del Popolo** is the heart of the famous Tridente (Neptune's trident), the nickname for Via di Ripetta, Via del Corso, and Via del Babuino. It's one of the largest squares in Rome. Porta del Popolo was once the most important entry gate to the city. On the edge of the square is a large fountain with sphinxes and statues representing the four seasons. The 79-foot-high Egyptian obelisk dates back to the 13th century B.C.

piazza del popolo, metro flaminio

(35) Legend has it that the **Santa Maria del Popolo** church was built on top of Emperor Nero's tomb. The story goes that a walnut tree grew in the much-hated emperor's grave, which was occupied by evil spirits shaped like black crows. The pope ended it all in the 11th century by chopping the tree down and building a chapel in its place. The church contains stunning sculptures by Raphael, Caravaggio, and Bernini.

piazza del popolo, www.santamariadelpopolo.it, t: 063610836, open mon-thu 7:15am-12:30pm & 4pm-7pm, fri-sat 7:30am-7pm, sun 7:30am-1:30pm & 4:30pm-7:30pm, free entrance, metro flaminio

FOOD & DRINK

⑧ The secluded green at **Casina del Lago** will make you feel miles away from the busy city traffic. The little house has stylish outdoor seating and a modern interior. It's a great place for a cappuccino or *aperitivo,* and for lunch.
viale dell'aranciera 2, www.caffeparana.it, t: 0685352623, summer open mon 9am-5pm, tue-sun 9am-9pm, winter open daily 9am-5pm, price sandwich €5, metro flaminio/bus viale san paolo del brasile

⑩ There is no better spot to enjoy the Spanish Steps than at **Il Palazzetto.** The benches around the terrace have comfortable red cushions. Though a *pizza margherita* will set you back a good €12, this idyllic location is well worth it. This is the perfect vantage point to enjoy all the hustle and bustle on the Steps.
vicolo del bottino 8, www.ilpalazzettoroma.com, t: 0669934560, open daily 1pm-9pm (depends greatly on the weather and season), price pizza €12, metro spagna

⑯ Lazio, the region surrounding Rome, produces a lot of wine. The regional administration opened modern wine bar **Palatium** to promote local wines and other products. Here you can also try regional dishes, all for very reasonable prices.
via frattina 94, www.enotecapalatium.com, t: 0669202132, open mon-sat 11am-11pm, price glass of wine €3, metro spagna

⑰ If you feel like having a healthy lunch, **Ginger** is the place to go. The walls of this restaurant are lined with heaps of fruit and hung with different kinds of ham. Help yourself to a sumptuous fruit salad, a plate of couscous, or a smoothie. Or enjoy a coffee and a slice of chocolate cake with ginger and lemon cream.
via borgognona 43-46, www.ginger.roma.it, t: 0669940836, open daily 10am-midnight, price salad €12, metro spagna

⑲ **Antico Caffè Greco** was established in 1760 by a Greek owner, and its regulars have included the likes of Goethe, Stendhal, Lord Byron, and Liszt. You can almost picture these illustrious figures sitting here in the original ornate interior. Sitting is expensive, though—we recommend ordering your espresso at the bar.
via dei condotti 86, www.anticocaffegreco.it, t: 066791700, open daily 9am-9pm, price sit-down espresso €6, metro spagna

㉑ People flock to **Pastificio** every day around 1pm. This old-fashioned pasta shop might look a little out of place in this upscale neighborhood, but it's incredibly popular—and with good reason. The sign outside that reads "tasting" is the only clue of what to expect. Two large plates full of steaming hot pasta are brought out and everyone is served a huge helping, along with water and wine. Yes, you'll be served on plastic plates, but at €4, who can complain?
via della croce 8, open daily 1pm-9pm, price pasta €4, metro spagna

㉒ The Pompi family has been making the best tiramisu in Rome since 1960 with dedication and a keen eye for detail, and constant research. Happy customers are the main focus at **Bar Pompi.** Of course you can opt for the classic recipe, but consider sampling one of their unique twists, such as strawberry flavor.
via della croce 82, www.barpompi.it, t: 0669941752, open daily 10am-10:30pm, price tiramisu €4, metro spagna

㉗ **Ad Hoc** is a simple yet welcoming restaurant, with cast iron chairs surrounded by wine bottles. Start with a tasting of local cheeses or charcuterie, then order some homemade pasta or gnocchi, or Tuscan beef. The staff is happy to recommend the perfect wine pairing.
via di ripetta 43, www.ristoranteadhoc.com, open daily 7pm-midnight, price €20, metro flaminio

㉚ The shelves on the wall at **Enoteca Buccone** bend under the weight of the wines and liqueurs. Have a seat at a marble table and order a glass with some nibbles on the side before you move on for dinner.
via di ripetta 19, www.enotecabuccone.com, t: 063612154, open mon-sat 12:30pm-3pm & fri-sat 7:30pm-10:30pm, sun 11am-6pm, price glass of wine €6, metro flaminio

㉛ **Il Brillo Parlante** is a classic *trattoria*. A few doors down, on the roof of Hotel Valadier, the same owner runs the fantastic **Hi-Res,** a restaurant specializing in seafood. The prices there are a bit higher, but the view from the bar with a drink in your hand is priceless.
via della fontanella 12-15, www.ilbrilloparlante.com, t: 063243334, trattoria open daily noon-12:30am, hi-res bar 12:30pm-1:30am, restaurant 7:30pm-11:30pm, price pasta at trattoria €10, metro flaminio

㉝ For those who think vegetarian food is stuffy, **Il Margutta Ristor Arte** has been proving them wrong since 1979. Their cooking is a testament to the fact that Italian cuisine can be equally fantastic sans meat or fish. Every afternoon, they offer a "green" brunch buffet in the spacious futuristic hall full of modern art. Dinner consists of fresh, creative dishes paired with wine.

via margutta 118, www.ilmargutta.it, t: 0632650577, open daily noon-3:30pm & 7pm-11:30pm, price pasta €12, metro spagna

SHOPPING

⑭ At **Sermoneta Gloves,** you can find a pair of gloves suited to your every need, be it a wedding, a drive, or just to keep your hands warm. The gloves are handmade from the best lamb leather in all colors and styles. Owner Giorgio Sermoneta's fame extends well beyond Rome—his gloves are also sold in New York and London.

piazza di spagna 61, www.sermonetagloves.com, t: 066791960, open mon-sat 9:30am-8pm, sun 10:30am-1pm & 2pm-7pm, metro spagna

⑱ After a visit to **Via dei Condotti,** fashionistas will need to head straight for their therapists. In and around this street is where all the famous fashion designers keep their shops: from Valentino to Armani and from Gucci to Prada. Even if you can't afford a designer handbag, just don your best outfit and pretend. That's what the Romans do, too.

via dei condotti, metro spagna

⑳ Italian designers possess the ability to transform even the most everyday kitchen utensils into something extraordinary. Everything at **c.u.c.i.n.a.** is black, white, chrome, or wood. Many of the items are more gadgets than anything else, but that won't make you feel any less tempted while perusing this shop.

via mario de'fiori 65, www.cucinastore.com, t: 066791275, open mon 3:30pm-7:30pm, tue-fri 10am-7:30pm, sat 10:30am-7:30pm, metro spagna

㉓ Italy is a country of opera, and music plays a very important role in Italian life. That's why **La Stanza della Musica** is a must for every music lover. Whether you're looking for a specific score, or a CD by your favorite Italian singer, there is plenty to pick and choose from in the "music chamber."

via dei greci 36, www.lastanzadellamusica.it, t: 063218874, open mon 3pm-7pm, tue-sat 10am-7pm, metro spagna

26) You'll find original designs in **Mia,** located in a former monastery. The store includes pieces like scrapwood furniture by Dutch designer Piet Hein Eek, paper crockery by Wasara and utensils by Eno, a lamp by Muuto, and planters by Bacsac. Extra inspiration can be found on their blog: *www.miamarket.blogspot.nl.*

via di ripetta 224, www.miaviadiripetta.com, t: 0697841892, open tue-sat 10:30am-2pm & 3:30pm-7:30pm, metro flaminio

28) Take a seat at **Olfattorio**'s bar for a "perfume tasting." Here you can sample different scents in a special smelling glass, and decide which one suits you best. The staff will explain all about the composition of their exclusive perfumes.

via di ripetta 34, www.olfattorio.it, t: 063612325, open daily 10:30am-7:30pm (closed sun in summer), metro flaminio

29) Soccer fans take note: You can score beautiful retro soccer shirts and shoes at **Old Soccer.** These are all replicas of the outfits players wore before clubs were sponsored starting in 1982. Of course you'll find many shirts of Italian soccer heroes, but the shop also carries some from other European legends. The floor is covered in grass and the walls are filled with newspaper articles about Italian victories.

via di ripetta 30, www.oldsoccer.it, t: 0696846111, open daily 10am-8pm, metro flaminio

MORE TO EXPLORE

1) During the 17th century, the park surrounding **Villa Borghese** was the back-yard of the influential Cardinal Scipio Borghese. Now it's a green park with high pine trees and a garden for all Romans. Besides going for a walk, you also can ride your bike here, have a picnic, and row on the lake.

entrance at viale san paolo del brasile, open daily, free entrance, metro flaminio/bus viale san paolo del brasile

② **Cinema dei Piccoli:** 785 square feet, 63 seats, one large screen, and a snack corner. When it opened its doors in 1934, the only films that were screened in this little wooden cinema were children's movies. Nowadays they also screen movies for grownups in the evenings—in their original language. The little house was proclaimed the smallest cinema in the world in 2005 by Guinness World Records.

largo marcello mastroianni 15, www.cinemadeipiccoli.it, t: 068553485, open daily, check website for times, price mon-fri €5, sat-sun €6, metro flaminio

④ The 30-acre zoo **Bioparco** opened its doors over a century ago, making it one of the oldest zoos in Europe. They have more than 1,000 animals—great for kids!

piazzale del giardino zoologico 1, www.bioparco.it, t: 06360821, open daily nov-mar 9:30am-5pm, apr-oct 9:30am-6pm (apr-sep sat-sun until 9pm), entrance €15, bus piazza thorwaldsen

⑤ From *Romeo & Juliet* to *King Lear,* the **Globe Theatre Roma** stages all the classics. Immerse yourself in the universal magic of the theater and the magical surroundings of Villa Borghese.

largo aqua felix, www.globetheatreroma.com, t: 060608, box office open 3pm-7pm, price standing room starting at €10, metro flaminio

⑨ The **Giardino del Pincio** lies at the top of the Pincio Hill. This estate was sold to the Pinci family after the Sack of Rome in 1527. The terrace offers spectacular views.

entrance piazzale napoleone i/viale delle magnolie, open daily, free entrance, metro spagna

㉜ **Via Margutta** has been a magnet for artists for centuries. Composers Stravinsky and Puccini and writer Truman Capote all came here to find inspiration. Filmmaker Fellini also loved this quiet little street. Nowadays not many artists can afford to live here, but the street is still lined with galleries. Have a look at #53, where a craftsman makes funny little signs that can be found all over the street.

via margutta, metro spagna

WALK 3

VATICAN, PRATI & PIAZZA NAVONA

ABOUT THE WALK

This walk consists of three parts, but you can follow each route separately. The Vatican alone is an experience that will set your head spinning. Prati, on the other hand, offers a more subdued experience, as this residential area is home to Rome's upper crust. The neighborhood surrounding Piazza Navona is more touristy and is characterized by authentic streets and restaurants.

THE NEIGHBORHOODS

The Vatican is an autonomous state in the middle of Rome with its own pharmacy, postal service, and police department. This city-state has some 800 inhabitants, making it the least populated country in the world. The Vatican makes up for this lack of residents with the sheer quantity of its art treasures. It has invested in art for centuries, and there is an abundant display of works at the **Musei Vaticani** and the **Basilica di San Pietro** (St. Peter's Basilica).

Prati, the neighborhood adjacent to the Vatican, is posh and upscale. Alongside straight streets you'll find stately apartment blocks and shops. For those who are uninterested in art, this neighborhood still has plenty to offer. **Via Cola di Rienzo** is especially great for shopping.

You'll find the impressive **Palazzo di Giustizia** on Piazza Cavour. But not every Roman is enchanted by the look of this ornamental courthouse. Almost adjacent lies **Castel Sant'Angelo.** This was once a mausoleum for imperial families, but is now home to part of the Museo Nazionale Romano. Bernini's angels on the **Ponte Sant'Angelo** guide visitors across the Tiber River.

Here narrow streets lead to **Piazza Navona,** once the athletic stadium of Emperor Domitian. This was a favorite spot for young aristocracy to visit during their Grand Tour of Europe during the second half of the 20th century. Nowadays many people come here for an afternoon stroll, to go out at night, or to have their portrait painted by one of the many street artists. You'll find all kinds of shops and places to eat on **Via del Governo Vecchio.** There are also many churches, fountains, and museums in this neighborhood. And the fun continues until well after sunset—you'll be amazed by the number of plastic cocktail glasses deposited carelessly on top of parked cars, especially around **Piazza del Fico.**

SHORT ON TIME? HERE ARE THE HIGHLIGHTS
+ BASILICA DI SAN PIETRO + MUSEI VATICANI + CAPPELLA SISTINA
+ CASTEL SANT'ANGELO + PIAZZA NAVONA

TIPS

// Perfect for first-time visitors
// Varied walk featuring art, religion, shops, and restaurants
// Take plenty of time to visit the Vatican

SIGHTS & ATTRACTIONS

① The colonnades on **Piazza San Pietro** are Bernini's masterpiece. He worked on them from 1655 until 1667, and people are still speechless when they see it. It consists of 284 columns divided into four rows. Look for the round stones between the obelisk and the fountains—here, the four rows seem to melt into one. The obelisk in the middle of the square is the oldest monument here. It was transported to Rome from Egypt in A.D. 36 and acts as a sundial—when the shadow reaches the white marble, it's the afternoon. The pope holds his weekly audience every Wednesday morning on this square. Free tickets can be obtained at the bronze gate in the colonnade on the right, up until a day in advance.

The **Basilica di San Pietro** (St. Peter's Basilica) was built on top of St. Peter's tomb and is the largest church in the world. It's nearly 450 feet high, from the ground up to the cross on top of the dome—three times as high as the Colosseum. The church's location was important even before the advent of Christianity, but it was Pope Julius II who ordered the construction of the current basilica in 1506. He called in the help of artists such as Bramante, Raphael, Peruzzi, Sangallo, and Michelangelo. The *Pietà* in the first chapel on the right is magnificent. It's the only sculpture Michelangelo ever signed: Nobody believed a young man could make anything this impressive.

The minute you see the view from the **Cupola di San Pietro** (the dome), you will forget all about the long hike up. You can walk up the whole way, or take an elevator to the first observation deck at 175 feet. Here you'll walk along a gallery at the base of the dome, high above the people in the church. You can reach the top via stairs inside the dome. Take your time if you decide to go up on foot— there are over 500 steps.

piazza san pietro, www.vatican.va, t: 0669883731, open daily apr-sep 7am-7pm, oct-march 7am-6:30pm, dome apr-sep 8am-6pm, oct-march 8am-5pm, free entrance to the church, dome €7 with elevator, €5 on foot, metro ottaviano/bus borgo sant'angelo or piazza risorgimento

② Plan on at least half a day to visit the **Musei Vaticani.** It's the largest, richest, and most impressive museum complex in the world. There are over 1,400

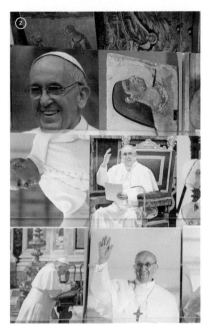

galleries filled with paintings, Greek and Roman sculptures, and Egyptian and Etruscan art. You can also visit the Missionary-Ethnological Museum and the Papal Apartments. The **Cappella Sistina,** or Sistine Chapel, is the highlight: Michelangelo's paintings and other frescoes displayed here are incredibly beautiful. Don't want to stand in line? Buy your ticket online (reservations €4).

viale vaticano, www.museivaticani.va, t: 0669883332, open mon-sat 9am-6pm (checkout until 4pm), last sun of the month 9am-2pm (free until 12:30pm), entrance €16, metro ottaviano/bus piazza risorgimento

⑮ With its elaborate decorations, straight lines, and sheer size, the **Palazzo di Giustizia** (Palace of Justice) was quickly nicknamed *palazzaccio* ("the ugly palace"). It took architect Calderini almost 22 years to build. It was finally finished in 1910.

lungotevere prati/piazza cavour 1, not open to the public, bus piazza cavour

⑰ **Castel Sant'Angelo** (Castle of the Holy Angel) was commissioned by the Roman Emperor Hadrian as a mausoleum for himself and his family, but since the fall of the Roman Empire, it has been used as a prison and a fortress. Nowadays it's a museum with a beautiful collection of ceramics, weapons, and Renaissance paintings. To see the structure of the building (and for a stunning view), walk from the cellar to the roof terrace. The hallway leading upward in a spiral dates back to Hadrian's time and is still partially accessible. On top of the fortress is a statue of an archangel. According to legend, he appeared to Pope Gregorius I as a sign that the plague had ended.

lungotevere castello 50, www.castelsantangelo.com, t: 066819111, open tue-sun 9am-7:30pm, entrance €10.50, metro lepanto/bus ponte vittorio emanuele ii

⑱ The **Ponte Sant'Angelo** is one of the most beautiful bridges crossing the Tiber River. Look up to see Bernini's angels. This pedestrian bridge was built in 1450 after the old Roman bridge had partially collapsed. The weight of the pilgrims making their way to Hadrian's tomb was too much for the original bridge to bear.

ponte sant'angelo, metro ottaviano/bus ponte vittorio emanuele ii

㉖ **Piazza Navona** is loved by artists, but mere mortals like to visit this square as well. Its oval shape is due to the fact that it was built on top of the remains of Emperor Domitian's athletic stadium. Parties and even tournaments would take place right here up until the 15th century, but then it was paved over and became a public square. You can still see some remains of the stadium north of the square and inside the crypt of Sant'Agnese in Agone church.

piazza navona, free entrance, bus corso del rinascimento

㉗ The **Fontana dei Quattro Fiumi,** in the middle of Piazza Navona, was designed by Bernini. The fountain is a symbol of the four most important rivers in the 17th century: the Nile, the Ganges, the Danube, and the Rio Plata. The story goes that Bernini covered the face of the Nile so he would not have to look at Sant'Agnese in Agone—the church designed by his rival, Borromini. Borromini, in return, placed one statue on the church facade that purposefully looks away from the fountain.

piazza navona, bus corso del rinascimento

㉘ According to legend, the **Sant'Agnese in Agone** church was built on the spot where Christian St. Agnes was put on display naked as punishment for not returning the advances of a pagan man who desired her. By a miracle, Agnes' hair suddenly grew very fast, allowing her to cover her naked body. She was tortured to death nonetheless. The church is a beautiful example of Borromini's Baroque architecture.

piazza navona, www.santagneseinagone.org, t: 0668192134, open tue-sat 9:30am-12:30pm & 3:30pm-7pm, sun & holidays 9am-1pm & 4pm-8pm, free entrance, bus corso del rinascimento

㉙ **Palazzo Altemps** houses Greek and Roman treasures from different collections, including the magnificent art collection of the Boncompagni Ludovisi family. Look for *The Galatian Suicide,* a stunning marble sculpture group from the 1st century B.C., a copy of the bronze original.

piazza di sant'apollinare 46, www.archeoroma.beniculturali.it, t: 0639967700, open tue-sun 9am-7:45pm, price €7 combo-ticket with palazzo massimo, terme di diocleziano, bus corso del rinascimento

FOOD & DRINK

④ After visiting the Vatican, you don't need to look far for lunch. At **200°** they bake bread to perfection in a 200 degree Celsius oven (400 degrees Fahrenheit). Choose from a plethora of sandwiches named for nearby sights, like the *Pièta* or *Colosseo*.

piazza del risorgimento 3, www.duecentogradi.it, t: 0639754129, open sun-thu 11am-2am, fri-sat 11am-4am, price sandwiches € 5, metro ottaviano

⑤ The outdoor seating with a view of St. Peter's Basilica is the main attraction at **Trattoria sul Tetto.** Everyone can enjoy a great fish dish or Roman pasta specialty on the top floor of the Orange Hotel.

via crescenzio 86, www.trattoriasultetto.it, t: 0668805550, open daily noon-midnight, price pasta €9, metro ottaviano/bus risorgimento

⑩ In the back of this bright space, you'll see kids or adults working on mosaics or arts and crafts. Besides a café and lunch room, **Art Studio Café** also offers all kinds of creative workshops. The place is filled with completed creations that are all for sale. You can also have coffee, lunch, or an *aperitivo.*

via dei gracchi 187a, www.artstudiocafe.it, t: 0632609104, open mon-sat 7:30am-8:30pm, price aperitivo €7, bus piazza del risorgimento/metro ottaviano

⑪ At **Mondo Arancina** you can indulge in a typical Sicilian speciality: *arancina* (little orange). Contrary to its name, this isn't a kind of fruit, but rather a deep-fried rice ball filled with meat, mozzarella cheese, and peas. This savory snack makes a great alternative lunch. Try one of the many different varieties, such as ham and cheese.

via marcantonio colonna 38, www.mondoarancina.it, t: 0697619213, open daily 9am-midnight, price €2.50, metro lepanto/bus piazza cavour

⑫ At **Sanacafé,** ask a food coach to help you improve your eating habits. You can also check the calories of each dish on their website beforehand. Whatever you choose, you're sure to get a healthy meal.

via pompeo magno 12, www.sanacafe.it, t: 0696035669, open mon-sat 9am-midnight, price pasta €12, metro lepanto/bus piazza cavour

⑭ At **L'Arcangelo** chef Arcangelo Dandini serves up creative interpretations of Roman dishes, such as warm octopus salad or deep-fried rabbit. Looking for a great dinner? Archangel is your answer.

via giuseppe gioacchino belli 59, t: 063210992, open mon-fri 1pm-2:30pm & 8pm-11pm, sat 8pm-11pm, price €25, metro lepanto/bus via cicerone

⑲ **Da Alfredo & Ada**'s namesakes are no longer here, but their son and granddaughter are now in charge of this restaurant. They don't have a menu, but the owner will let you know their daily specials—*pasta all'amatriciana*, for example, or veal stew. The food is typically Roman: simple and very affordable.

via dei banchi nuovi 14, t: 06878842, open mon-fri noon-3pm & 7pm-10:30pm, price €7, bus piazza chiesa nuova

㉑ Delicious pizza awaits you at **Mimì e Cocò,** so find a spot out on their cozy terrace (heated in the winter) and enjoy. They give you something to snack on with your glass of wine, and if you want to dine here, you may get a *limoncello* on the house after dinner.

via del governo vecchio 72, www.mimiecoco.com, t: 0668210845, open daily 9:30am-2am, price glass of wine €5, bus piazza chiesa nuova

㉓ In the long and narrow **Cul de Sac** you can choose from over 1,500 different kinds of wine, bubbly, and *grappa*. They have the standard small dishes: Cheese and sausage, but also hummus and quiches. It's always buzzing and fun.

piazza pasquino 73, www.enotecaculdesacroma.it, t: 0668801094, open daily noon-12:30am, price glass of wine from €4, bus corso del rinascimento

㉚ Put on your best sunglasses, order a cappuccino, and engage in some serious people watching at **Antico Caffè della Pace.** You never know who you'll see at this celebrity hotspot that's been in business since 1891. Sitting outside in front of their overgrown facade, you'll feel like a star in your own right.

via della pace 3-7, www.caffedellapace.it, t: 066861216, open mon 3:30pm-2pm, tue-sun 8:30am-2am, price coffee €3, bus piazza chiesa nuova/corso del rinascimento

㉛ If you have the opportunity to eat lunch in the loggia of a 15th-century monastery, food may not be your main priority. But it just so happens that the food at

the *caffetteria/bistrot* of the **Chiostro del Bramante** is outstanding. This is a great option for brunch on weekends, with a serene view of the courtyard.

arco della pace 5, www.chiostrodelbramante.it, t: 0668809036, open mon-fri 10am-8pm, sat-sun 10am-9pm (lunch 11:30am-3pm, sat-sun brunch 10am-3pm), price salad €8, bus piazza chiesa nuova/corso del rinascimento

(32) The chef at **NO.AU** is also known as MacGyver: You need to be pretty resourceful to prepare such delicious food in a 75-square-foot kitchen with no stove! The name is a nod to their natural and organic ingredients.

piazza di montevecchio 16a, www.noauroma.wordpress.com, t: 0645652770, open tue-thu 6pm-1am, fri-sun noon-1am, price hamburger €10, bus piazza chiesa nuova/ corso del rinascimento

(34) The credo at **Circus** speaks volumes about this bar: "Rock & Roll, Paranoia, Cigarettes & Alcohol." This Italian café is perfect for Britpop aficionados.

via della vetrina 15, www.circusroma.it, t: 0697619258, open daily 10am-2am, price beer €5, bus piazza chiesa nuova/corso del rinascimento

③⑤ **Gelateria del Teatro** sells ice cream in unique flavor combinations: white chocolate with basil or strawberries and champagne are just two of the options you'll find here. They also have refreshing *granita* (shaved ice from Sicily). Around the corner you'll find the affiliated **Pizza del Teatro.** Don't expect to find pasta, but they do make a great *pizza cacio en pepe.*

via dei coronari 65, t: 0645474880, open daily noon-midnight, price €2.50, bus via paola/piazza chiesa nuova

SHOPPING

⑥ If you're a fan of Italian fashion labels but your bank account isn't, **Gente Outlet** is the place to go. They sell all the famous brands for a fraction of the original price. Many items are last season, but hey, Prada is Prada!

via cola di rienzo 246, www.genteroma.com, t: 0668135000, open tue-sat 10am-7pm, mon & sun 11am-2pm & 3:30pm-7:30pm, metro ottaviano

⑧ **Barbara Guidi** was once a film historian, but now mostly studies textiles. Her shop is full of her own fashion designs—basics with unique details, plus bags and jewelry. Barbara is known for her eccentric headdresses. This is a great place to shop if you want to give your party outfit a little twist.

via dei gracchi 106, www.barbaraguidi.com, t: 0698936884, open mon 3:30pm-7:30pm, tue-sat 10:30am-1:30pm & 3:30pm-7:30pm, metro ottaviano/bus piazza del risorgimento

⑨ **Castroni** is a local chain of old-fashioned delicatessen shops filled with Italian specialties, plus some from other countries like Japan, Greece, and Thailand. Coconut milk and soy sauce are no longer unique, but were hard to find in the 1950s. Today, people go to Castroni for the vintage interior, the coffee, and other Italian goodies.

via cola di rienzo 196-198, www.castroni.it, t: 066874383, open mon-sat 7:45am-8pm, sun 9:30am-8pm, metro ottaviano/bus piazza del risorgimento

⑬ **40 Gradi** is run by two brothers who travel the world to source the coolest streetwear clothing. Their collection includes punk fashion items from London, obscure Japanese clothing labels, and vintage brandname athletic wear. The store is chaotic and fun, and even has free beer on tap!

via virgilio 1, www.quarantagradi.it, open mon-sat 10am-8pm, metro lepanto/bus via cicerone

(20) **Kolby** sells some women's clothing, but this cool fashion shop with high ceilings and a large marble countertop caters mostly to men. You'll find basic clothes made from coarse linen, chunky knitwear, and sturdy belts. They also have their own fashion line.

via del governo vecchio 63-65, www.kolby.it, t: 0668803732, open mon-tue 11am-8pm, wed-sat 10am-8pm, sun noon-7:30pm, bus corso del rinascimento

(22) **Zou Zou** is a refreshing erotic shop. The fitting room is painted top to bottom with sexy images, and if you organize a bachelorette party, you can model three titillating outfits for your friends. This is a classy shop with sexy lingerie and other fun gadgets to spice up your love life.

vicolo della cancelleria 9a, www.zouzoustore.com, t: 066892176, open mon 2pm-7:30pm, tue-sat 11am-7:30pm, bus corso del rinascimento

(24) Strategic Business Unit, or **S.B.U.,** sells menswear. They carry jeans mostly, but if you're looking for a nice Italian jacket with fine European tailoring, this is a great place to find one. Everything is designed and produced in Italy. They have a celebrity clientele.

via di san pantaleo 68, www.sbu.it, t: 0668802547, open mon-sat 10am-7:30pm, bus corso del rinascimento

(33) The name **Retrò** says it all: This shop sells furniture and accessories from the 1940s, '50s, '60s, and '70s. You'll see things like psychedelic glass objects, bakelite telephones, and futuristic chairs. Retro lovers come here to search for objects from Italian and Scandinavian designers. It's the perfect place to look for a unique piece for your living room.

piazza del fico 20-21, www.retrodesign.it, t: 0668192746, open mon-sat 11am-1pm & 4pm-8pm, bus piazza chiesa nuova/corso del rinascimento

MORE TO EXPLORE

③ If you want to visit the **Giardini Vaticani** (Vatican gardens), you have to make reservations online two days in advance. The tour takes approximately two hours and you start close to the entrance of the Musei Vaticani. You can also book a bus tour at Roma Cristiana at the beginning of Via della Conciliazione. The meticulously maintained gardens around the former summer residence of pope Pius IV are a green oasis within the walls of the Vatican.

viale vaticano, www.museivaticani.va, t: 0669883145, tours mon-tue & thu-sat, entrance €32, metro ottaviano/bus piazza risorgimento

⑦ **Mercato Rionale** opened its doors in 1930, and became a popular meeting point for the people living in the upscale Prati neighborhood. Despite the overwhelming competition of large supermarkets and retail chains, this market is still alive and kicking. You can buy vegetables, fruit, fish, and meat in this charming hall.

via cola di rienzo 53, open mon-sat 6:30am-7:30pm, bus piazza risorgimento/metro ottaviano

⑯ The **Parco Adriano** surrounding Hadrian's mausoleum was built on two levels. People walk their dogs and children run around on the lower level. The upper level, with its benches overlooked by large trees, is a great place to unwind. Book markets and concerts are held here in the summer. The views of the walls of Castel Sant'Angelo are impressive.

castel sant'angelo, open dusk till dawn, free entrance, metro ottaviano/bus piazza chiesa nuova

㉕ In 2011 a group of artists occupied an 18th-century theater to protest the political developments that were crippling the arts and culture. It's been called **Teatro Valle Occupato** ever since, and to this day you can see some very unique shows here. Come see for yourself, and have a drink in the foyer to support their cause.

via del teatro valle 21, www.teatrovalleoccupato.it, t: 0668803794, opening hours vary, check the website, bus corso vittorio emanuele ɪɪ

WALK 4

CAMPO DE' FIORI, GHETTO & TRASTEVERE

ABOUT THE WALK

The longest walk in this guide, this route is characterized by churches, museums, and prominent palazzi. But those with a taste for food and casual conversation will love this walk, because there are many cozy cafés and great restaurants along the way.

THE NEIGHBORHOODS

Via Giulia and **Via di Monserrato** are arguably the most beautiful Renaissance streets in the city. They culminate at the **Palazzo Farnese,** home to the French embassy. Nearby is the always-lively **Campo de' Fiori** ("Field of Flowers"). Early in the morning, market vendors sell their wares and shoppers fill up the square later on. At night, Romans and tourists alike come here to mingle and party.

There are plenty of restaurants, from trendy bars to traditional *trattorias,* and there is no shortage of shops, either. **Via dei Baullari** and **Via dei Giubbonari** feature a great mix of casual and chic stores.

The beautiful **Piazza Mattei,** with its Turtle Fountain, leads to the heart of the ghetto: the Jewish district between the Capitol and the Tiber River. It is one of Rome's most authentic neighborhoods. Today's Jewish residents still wish each other a peaceful Sabbath on Friday nights. Restaurants are closed on Fridays, but throughout the rest of the week, people come here to enjoy the famous *carciofi alla giudia* (fried artichokes). Roman-Jewish cuisine is very distinct because this ghetto was walled in for centuries.

Rome's city island, Isola Tiberina, leads to **Trastevere,** the neighborhood on the "other side" of the Tiber River. In some spots this historic district feels almost like a small village because it is so quiet and calm. Other parts are mobbed by tourists, and it's especially alive and bustling at night. Despite these changes, the original *Trasteverini* take great pride in their neighborhood.

The botanical gardens and **Villa Farnesina** are attractions on the outskirts of the neighborhood. The **Gianicolo** (Janiculum Hill), towering high above the rest of the neighborhood, is great for a walk. A canon is fired here every day at noon.

SHORT ON TIME? HERE ARE THE HIGHLIGHTS
+ VIA GIULIA + PALAZZO SPADA + PIAZZA MATTEI + SANTA MARIA IN TRASTEVERE + GIANICOLO

TIPS
// Apart from Gianicolo Hill, this walk is also perfect as a bike ride
// This walk can be split in half
// Reverse the route if you want to hear the canon at noon

SIGHTS & ATTRACTIONS

④ The French **Palazzo Farnese** was commissioned in 1514, but 60 years passed before it was completed. A succession of architects worked on it, including Michelangelo. The granite tubs, now located in the square, were once used in the Baths of Caracalla. You can tour the palace, but you need to book far in advance.

piazza farnese, www.ambafrance-it.org, t: 060608, only open by reservation, www.inventerrome.com, visits on mon, wed & fri, entrance €5, bus/tram via arenula

⑤ **Palazzo Spada** houses the painting collection of cardinal Bernardino Spada, including works by Guido Reni, Tiziano, and others. Don't miss Borromini's famous perspective trick: There was no money or room for a long arcade, so the architect thought of an ingenious solution. No time to go inside? Go into the courtyard and peer through the wooden window frames on the left to see this optical illusion.

piazza capo di ferro 13, www.galleriaborghese.it, t: 0632810, open wed-mon 8:30am-7:30pm, entrance €5, bus/tram via arenula

⑭ The four temples of **Area Sacra dell'Argentina** are the oldest in Rome. They were discovered in the 20th century during construction work. Some archaeologists believe this is the original site of the Curia of Pompey, where Julius Caesar was murdered. The Area is also known as the "cat forum" because of the many stray cats that live here.

largo di torre argentina, www.romancats.com, t: 0668805611, cat rescue open daily noon-5:30pm, voluntary contribution is appreciated, bus largo di torre argentina

⑮ The museum of the **Crypta Balbi** shows how Rome has changed throughout the centuries. It starts with Imperial times, when the theater and crypt of general Balbi stood here. Parts of the crypt were later used to build other structures.

via delle botteghe oscure 31, t: 066977671, open tue-sun 9am-7:45pm, entrance €7 (combo-ticket with palazzo altemps), bus largo di torre argentina

(16) The **Chiesa del Gesù** (full name: Chiesa del Santissimo Nome di Gesù) was built between 1568 and 1584 as the main church of the Jesuit order. Ignatius of Loyola, the order's founder, is buried inside the church. His richly decorated grave is located in a chapel on the left. Tip: Swing by the doorman on the right-hand side of the entrance and ask if you can see the Stanza di Sant'Ignazio—it's the epitome of *trompe-l'oeil.*

piazza del gesù, www.chiesadelgesu.org, t: 06697001, open daily 7am-12:30pm & 4pm-7:45pm, free entrance, bus largo di torre argentina

(17) On the elegant **Piazza Mattei,** you'll find the beautiful Fontana delle Tartarughe (Turtle Fountain). The story goes that a young nobleman with financial troubles had this fountain built overnight to impress the father of the woman he wished to marry. Next, he bricked up the window from which he and his beloved would view the fountain with the words: "Close this window, as the way we saw it, only we saw it." You can still see the bricked-up window on the second floor of #18. It's more likely, however, that Giacomo della Porta designed the fountain in the late 16th century. Bernini added the turtles later.

piazza mattei, bus largo di torre argentina

(23) Julius Caesar began the construction of the **Teatro di Marcello** (Theater of Marcellus), one of the largest theaters in ancient Rome, and Augustus finished it around 12 B.C. It was never used for gladiator fights or sports matches. Augustus dedicated the theater to his nephew Marcellus, who died at a young age. Now it's home to rich Romans.

entrance via foro piscario (via del portico d'ottavia)/via del teatro di marcello, open daily winter 9am-6pm, summer 9am-7pm, free entrance, bus piazza venezia

(24) The **Sinagoga** and **Museo Ebraico di Roma** are located in the heart of the Jewish neighborhood. With a history dating back over 2,000 years, this is the oldest Jewish community in Europe. The Roman Jews were persecuted repeatedly, especially during the 16th century when anti-Semitic pope Paul IV forced them to live within the walls of the cramped and unsanitary ghetto.

lungotevere de' cenci, www.museoebraico.roma.it, t: 066840061, open winter sun-thu 10am-4:15pm, fri 9am-1:15pm, summer sun-thu 10am-5:15pm, fri 10am-3:15pm, entrance €11, bus largo di torre argentina

㉘ The **Basilica di Santa Cecilia** was built in the 9th century on the spot where, legend has it, the house of the holy Cecilia once stood. A devout Christian, she was sentenced to death by being boiled alive in her own bath. For three days she sat in the hot tub, but when nothing happened, she was sentenced to beheading instead. After the executioner struck her three times on the neck with a sword, she still wouldn't die and ended up living another three days, singing during her entire ordeal. Today she is the patron saint of musicians.

piazza di santa cecilia 22, www.benedettinesantacecilia.it, t: 0645492739, open daily 9:15am-12:45pm & 4pm-6pm, free entrance, tram viale di trastevere

㉜ **Tempietto del Bramante,** a cute little Renaissance temple, was erected at the start of the 16th century by Bramante. The king of Spain commissioned the architect to commemorate the martyrdom of St. Peter that, according to some, took place right here.

piazza di san pietro in montorio 2, www.sanpietroinmontorio.it, t: 065813940, open mon-fri 8:30am-noon & 3pm-4pm, sat-sun 8am-noon, free entrance, bus/tram viale di trastevere

㉞ **Santa Maria in Trastevere** church, dating back to the 4th century, is believed to be Rome's first Christian church. Legend has it that in A.D. 38 a stream of oil *(fons olei)* flowed from the ground for an entire day, just right of the main altar. This was interpreted as a sign of the imminent coming of Christ. The current building was constructed in the 12th century, as were the golden mosaics on the facade that depict Mary and baby Jesus. The church was built with materials stolen from the Baths of Caracalla. The columns date back to antiquity.

piazza santa maria in trastevere, t: 065814802, open daily 7:30am-9pm (hours different in aug), free entrance, tram viale di trastevere

㊱ In a cozy corner of Trastevere, near the botanical gardens (that are also worth a visit), lies **Galleria Corsini.** This museum displays part of the collection of the Galleria Nazionale d'Arte Antica: paintings from the 16th and 17th centuries by Italian artists and others, such as Rubens. The most beautiful room is that of Queen Christina of Sweden, who died here in 1689.

via della lungara 10, www.galleriacorsini.beniculturali.it, t: 0668802323, open wed-mon 8:30am-7:30pm, entrance €5, tram viale di trastevere

(37) At **Villa Farnesina** you'll find Renaissance architecture, geometric gardens, and frescoes by Peruzzi and Raphael. The owner, a wealthy banker named Agostini Chigi, commissioned frescoes of his naked mistress for one of the rooms, and it's thought that his wife modeled for a mural in the bedroom called *The Marriage of Alexander and Roxana.*

via della lungara 230, www.villafarnesina.it, t: 0668027268, open mon-sat 9am-2pm, entrance €6, tram viale di trastevere

FOOD & DRINK

(2) **Il Goccetto** ("the sip") is located in an 18th-century building. They serve over 800 types of wine and have been an institution in the neighborhood for over 30 years. Have some cheese and *prosciutto* to complement your wine.

via dei banchi vecchi 14, www.ilgoccetto.com, t: 066864268, open mon 6:30pm-midnight, tue-sat 11:30am-2:30pm & 6:30pm-midnight, price glass of wine €5, bus piazza chiesa nuova

(6) **Da Sergio** is a typical *trattoria* famous for its *carbonara,* but their display cases are filled with other fresh and delicious foods. Don't forget to finish with a glass of the Roman liquor called *L'incendio di Nerone.* Whatever you eat will go down better with a sip of the "flame of Nero."

vicolo delle grotte 27, t: 066864293, open mon-sat noon-3:30pm & 6pm-midnight, price pasta €10, bus via arenula

(9) **Grappolo d'Oro Zampanò** is an old-fashioned *trattoria* that has reinvented itself. The chef takes Roman classics and creatively reinterprets them with an extra twist. Specialties include lamb and a pecorino cheese flan.

piazza della cancelleria 80-84, www.hosteriagrappolodoro.it, t: 066897080, open mon-fri 12:45pm-3pm & 7pm-11:30pm, sat 12:30pm-3pm & 7pm-11:30pm, sun 12:45pm-3:30pm & 7pm-11pm, price pasta €9.50, bus largo di torre argentina

(10) Bakery **Il Fornaio** is guaranteed to make your mouth water, with over 30 different types of cookies and 20 kinds of cake, as well as various breads, pizzas and paninis. The *pizza bianca*—pizza with no sauce—is a popular choice. Order

yours with *mortadella* (Italian sausage). Make sure you leave some room for a sweet and delicious dessert.

via dei baullari 5-7, t: 0668803947, open daily 7am-midnight, bus largo di torre argentina

⑪ At **Hostaria Costanza** you'll be seated amongst the ruins of a Roman amphitheater—the Theater of Pompey. It is said that Julius Caesar was murdered here. On the menu are some delicious main courses, but their *antipasti* come highly recommended as well—pancakes with mushrooms and truffle or chicken liver with mascarpone cheese.

piazza del paradiso 63-65, www.hostariacostanza.it, t: 066861717, open mon-sat 12:30pm-3pm & 7:30pm-11:30pm, price pasta €12, bus corso vittorio emanuele ii

⑬ For three generations now bakery **Roscioli** has provided Romans with the best *pizza bianca* and breads. But the *salumeria/vineria* of the same name, just around the corner and belonging to the family's youngest sons, is proving an even bigger hit. They sell fantastic cheeses, hams, and wines. Order the *burrata,* a cheese that melts in your mouth. They also offer fun tasting sessions. Reservations are a must, especially for dinner.

via dei giubbonari 21, www.salumeriaroscioli.com, t: 066875287, bakery open mon-sat 8am-8pm, wine bar 12:30pm-4pm & 7pm-midnight, price pasta €14, bus largo di torre argentina

⑳ More and more small breweries are opening in Rome, all with specialty beers. **Open Baladin** has more than 140 varieties on their menu, and they serve homemade potato chips and hamburgers. The staff is cheerful and the vibe is laidback.

via degli specchi 6, www.openbaladin.com, t: 066838989, open daily noon-2am, price beer €5, bus largo di torre argentina

㉑ You have to try a kosher meal when you visit the ghetto. **Ba'ghetto** has two nice family restaurants on the same street, both offering a large variety of dishes made with either dairy or meat.

via del portico d'ottavia 2a and 57, www.kosherinrome.it, t: 0668892868, open sun-thu noon-11pm, fri noon-3pm, sat 9:30am-11pm, price pasta €9, bus/tram largo di torre argentina

㉖ You can choose your own fresh fish at **Fish Market,** just like at a real market. The menu is already on the table—put a check mark by the dishes you would like and pay for your meal. Drinks can be ordered at the separate beverage counter. This is a refreshing approach to Italian dining.

vicolo della luce, www.fishmarket-roma.com, t: 3203910934, open daily 7:30pm-1am, sat-sun 1pm-3:30pm, price salmon burger €8, bus/tram viale di trastevere

㉙ **Ai Marmi** is not the best place for a romantic dinner: Rows of hungry guests line the street, waiting for a scarce spot at a table. The tables are made of white marble, which is why this popular pizza joint is commonly known by its nickname *"l'obitorio"* ("the morgue"). It's hectic and noisy, and the wait staff like to keep things moving, but it's full of Roman charm.

viale di trastevere 53-55, t: 065800919, open thu-tue 7pm-2am, price pizza €7, tram viale di trastevere

㉚ **Baylon Cafè,** located on a quiet street in the middle of the busy Trastevere neighborhood, is a great place for a lovely aperitif. Around cocktail hour they

serve a mini-menu for €5 that is so generous you'll probably want to skip dinner. Perfect to enjoy with a glass of wine.

via di san francesco a ripa 151, t: 065814275, open daily 6:30am-2am, price aperitif €5, bus/tram viale di trastevere

(31) **Fata Morgana** is an innovative *gelateria* in stiff competition with the more established ice-cream shops in town. Try the Punch Paradise or coconut with Saint James rum. They use no dyes or preservatives.

piazza san cosimato, www.gelateriafatamorgana.com, t: 065803615, open daily noon-midnight, price €2.50, bus/tram viale di trastevere

(33) The walls of **Trattoria de Gli Amici** are decorated with artwork made by mentally disabled people who also work in the restaurant together with professionals and volunteers. As the name suggests, (*amici* means "friends"), the vibe is friendly and amicable and they serve up some very original dishes, such as ravioli with nettle and hazelnut pesto. It comes highly recommended, especially on this square where most places are of mediocre quality.

piazza di sant'egidio 6, www.trattoriadegliamici.org, t: 065806033, open daily 12:30pm-3pm & 7:30pm-11:30pm, price pasta €11, tram viale di trastevere

SHOPPING

(8) Hats, striped trousers, and flowery dresses: The children's apparel at **Rachele** is colorful and eclectic. Her foldable care bag is especially popular. Suitable for kids age 6 and under.

vicolo del bollo 6, www.racheleartchildrenswear.it, t: 066864975, open tue-sat 10:30am-2pm & 3:30pm-7:30pm, bus piazza chiesa nuova/campo de' fiori

(12) Back in 1972, Elisa Nepi's parents opened the beautiful shop **Ibiz,** inspired by the tanneries on Ibiza. Now Elisa runs the shop and produces handcrafted bags, belts, sandals, and wallets with mostly Tuscan leather in the little workshop in the back of the store. Ibiz offers exceptional service and a lifetime guarantee.

via dei chiavari 39, www.ibizroma.it, t: 0668307297, open mon-sat 10am-7:30pm, bus/tram via arenula

(18) **Il Museo del Louvre** boasts a collection of over 30,000 intriguing vintage photographs. Some come from famous photographers or agencies, but most were shot by anonymous amateurs. Check out the endless assortment of family shots, cityscapes, and fashion shoots. Two doors down is an antique shop with more oddities and collectibles, including letters, notepads, and old books.

via della reginella 8a, www.ilmuseodellouvre.com, t: 0668807725, open mon-sat 10:30am-2pm & 3pm-7pm, bus teatro marcello/largo di torre argentina

(19) The display cases at **Beppe e i Suoi Formaggi** ("Beppe and his cheeses") are filled to the brim with dozens of cheeses, whilst in the back of the store whole cheeses mature in a glass, climate-controlled chamber. Purchase some exciting cheeses for a picnic, or sit down in the shop itself for a cheese tasting accompanied with wine.

via santa maria del pianto 9a, www.beppeeisuoiformaggi.it, t: 0668192210, open mon-sat 9am-10:30pm, bus largo di torre argentina

(22) Kitchen fanatics will feel like they've entered heaven once they descend the stairs at **Leone Limentani.** This has been the go-to store for everything cooking-related since 1820. Its endless halls are crammed with kitchenware, tableware, crystal, and cooking gadgets. The goods are often boxed up, but you'll get a better deal here than in other upscale kitchen shops.

via del portico d'ottavia 47, www.limentani.com, t: 0668307000, open summer mon-sat 9am-1pm & 4pm-8pm, winter 9am-1pm & 3:30pm-7:30pm, bus largo di torre argentina

(27) Alberto is the craftsman behind the elegant tie shop **La Cravatta su Misura,** but the business is now run by his daughter. Dozens of bolts of silk lie in wait to be turned into bespoke ties. They also make bowties and woolen scarves.

via di santa cecilia 12, www.lacravattasumisura.it, t: 0689016941, open mon-fri 10am-7pm, sat 10am-2pm, tram viale di trastevere

(35) One of the best places for eyeglasses in Rome is **Occhio al Vicolo.** The interior is bright orange and they sell sunglasses from well-known brands for extremely competitive prices. They offer great service and stay open until late.

vicolo del cinque 7, www.occhioalvicolo.it, t: 0658334242, open daily 10:30am-midnight, tram viale di trastevere

MORE TO EXPLORE

①Rome is full of enchanting little streets, but **Via Giulia** is unquestionably one of the prettiest. Stroll past more than half a mile of churches, antique stores, art galleries, and government buildings, with hardly any traffic. This Renaissance street was designed by Bramante as a quick-access road for pilgrims on their way to the Vatican.

via giulia, bus piazza chiesa nuova

③ **Via di Monserrato** was home to many courtesans in the Middle Ages, but Michelangelo lived here as well. It was also the place where Beatrice Cenci was held prisoner before she was beheaded for killing her father (he had abused her). Nowadays the street is home to delightful boutiques (selling everything from jewelry to furniture and movie posters). Check out #117 with the cryptic text *TRAHIT SUA QUEMQUE VOLUPTAS:* "Everyone is driven by their own lust."

via di monserrato, piazza chiesa nuova

⑦ **Campo de' Fiori** is one of the most vibrant squares in Rome. Early in the morning the market vendors set up their stalls, selling vegetables, fruits, and flowers until around 2pm, when the square slowly transforms into a place to go out.

piazza campo de' fiori, bus piazza chiesa nuova

㉖ In the summertime the banks of the Tiber River and those of the **Isola Tiberina** (Tiber Island) are filled with stalls and bars. The busy Fatebenefratelli Hospital works overtime year-round. The Ponte Fabricio, stretching from the ghetto to the island, is the only ancient Roman bridge that is still completely intact, dating back to 62 B.C.

isola tiberina, bus largo di torre argentina

WALK 5

TERMINI, MONTI & FORI IMPERIALI

ABOUT THE WALK

This shorter walk begins and ends with a visit to a museum and archaeological sites, leading you past several other important sights. If history doesn't interest you, start at sight number 7 of this walk, in the charming Monti neighborhood.

THE NEIGHBORHOODS

The area around Termini Central Station was once the largest bath complex in Rome. The shape of Piazza della Repubblica is reminiscent of this time, and museums **Terme di Diocleziano** and **Palazzo Massimo** feature everything about its history. Palazzo Massimo is adjacent to Viminal Hill, one of the Seven Hills of Rome.

Another hill in this neighborhood is Esquiline, with the Santa Maria Maggiore basilica as its beacon. This is also where you'll find the **San Pietro in Vincoli** church, which houses the famous statue of Moses by Michelangelo.

Monti was once a neighborhood filled with brothels, cheap taverns, and craftsmen's workshops. The studios are still here, though they are now occupied by artists and designers. The taverns have been transformed into modern wine bars and the cobbled streets are lined with boutiques and trattorias. Together, the combination of dilapidated buildings and hipster scenery forms a picture-perfect movie backdrop.

The first thing you'll notice on Piazza Venezia is the **Vittoriano:** this impressive white building is often sardonically referred to as "the wedding cake." On Capitoline Hill you'll find the **Musei Capitolini,** with no less than 1,300 works of art, many of which are antique statues. **Piazza del Campidoglio,** where the museum complex is located, was designed by Michelangelo and offers a stunning view of the Roman Forum.

Busy Via dei Fori Imperiali, built against Caelian Hill, leads from Piazza Venezia to the **Colosseum.** The fearless gladiators who fought here in ancient times have appealed to our collective imagination for centuries. Nowadays you can have your picture taken with one of the many Roman men in gladiator costumes that frequent this area. Of course, they don't hold a candle to their ancestral counterparts, but it's still a fun memento of your visit to the Eternal City.

SHORT ON TIME? HERE ARE THE HIGHLIGHTS
**+ PALAZZO MASSIMO + BASILICA DI SANTA MARIA MAGGIORE
+ MERCATI DI TRAIANO + PIAZZA DEL CAMPIDOGLIO + COLOSSEO**

TIPS

// A great combination of history and current events
// Perfect for those who have visited Rome before
// Park your bike in Monti, the rest of this route is very bikeable

SIGHTS & ATTRACTIONS

② There's not much left of the once-mighty **Terme di Diocleziano** (Baths of Diocletian). Over 3,000 people used to bathe here simultaneously, which is twice the capacity of the Baths of Caracalla. Later, the large *exedra* was transformed into Piazza della Repubblica, and the main building became the Santa Maria degli Angeli e dei Martiri church. The museum has a beautiful archaeological collection.

viale enrico de nicola 79, www.archeoroma.beniculturali.it, t: 0639967700, open tue-sun 9am-7:30pm, entrance €7 (combo-ticket with palazzo altemps and crypta), bus/metro termini

③ **Palazzo Massimo** will captivate you with five centuries of classic art, such as the world-famous Roman marble copy of *Discobolus* dating back to the 2nd century and modeled after the Greek bronze original by Miro. Also breathtaking are the murals from the country house of Emperor Augustus' wife Livia.

piazza dei cinquecento 67, www.archeoroma.beniculturali.it, t: 0639967700, open tue-sun 9am-7:45pm, entrance €7 (combo-ticket with palazzo altemps and crypta), bus/metro termini

④ **Piazza della Repubblica** used to be called Piazza Esedra, after the large semi-circular niche that was part of the Baths of Diocletian. Over 150 years ago, during the unification of Italy, architect Gaetano Koch was commissioned to revamp this square. He paid homage to the ancient shapes with two neoclassical colonnades. The Fontana delle Naiadi (Fountain of Water Nymphs) was designed by Alessandro Guerrieri in 1885.

piazza della repubblica, free entrance

⑤ Close to Termini station, on Esquiline Hill, you'll find the **Basilica di Santa Maria Maggiore.** Legend has it that pope Liberius built this church in the 4th century A.D. after dreaming about the Virgin Mary. Pope Sixtus III rebuilt the basilica a century later. The gilded coffered ceiling is particularly beautiful. In the back of the church is Bernini's grave. At 240 feet, the bell tower is the highest in the city.

piazza di santa maria maggiore, www.vatican.va, t: 0669886800, open daily 7am-7pm, free entrance, metro termini/vittorio emanuele

⑨ The **San Pietro in Vincoli** church was built in the 5th century. This is where the chains (Latin: *vincola*) used on St. Peter during his imprisonment in the Mamertine Prison in Rome were kept. The church is divided into three naves, separated by 20 antique columns. The tomb of Pope Julius II, who commissioned the church, is the highlight of the basilica. Here, Michelangelo worked from 1513 to 1515 on the massive statue of Moses, which is twice the size of a real man.

piazza san pietro in vincoli 4/a, t: 0697844952, open daily 8am-12:30pm & 3pm-6pm, free entrance, metro cavour

㉖ During the reign of Emperor Trajan at the start of the 2nd century, Rome underwent a period of growth and prosperity. The **Mercati di Traiano** gives us a glimpse of what daily life was like back then. Imagine what this enormous complex of 150 shops and offices used to look like back in the day, when fish merchants would hawk their wares and drive their carts over the cobblestoned streets. You'll have a fantastic view of the market halls and Fori Imperiali from Via Alessandrina.

via iv novembre 94, www.mercatiditraiano.it, t: 060608, open daily 9:30am-7:30pm, entrance €14 (also provides entrance to the museo dei fori imperiali), bus piazza venezia

㉗ The **Colonna di Traiano** (Trajan's Column) is decorated with no less than 2,500 figures divided over 25 large marble blocks. The reliefs tell of the battles Emperor Trajan waged in Dacia (today's Romania). With his spoils of war, Trajan was able to finance the construction of his forum. The column is as high as the hill that had to be excavated to build Trajan's Market.

via dei fori imperiali, bus/tram piazza venezia

㉚ Mussolini used **Palazzo Venezia** as his headquarters. He delivered many of his speeches from the balcony overlooking Piazza Venezia. In the 16th and 17th centuries, the building was home to the embassy of the Republic of Venice. Now it's a museum with art that was collected during that period, including paintings, tapestries, and portraits (look at the ladies' complicated hairdos).

via del plebiscito 118, www.museopalazzovenezia.beniculturali.it, open tue-sun 8:30am-7:30pm, entrance €5, bus/tram piazza venezia

㉜ Capitoline Hill is the smallest of the Seven Hills, but just as mighty. The **Piazza del Campidoglio** at the top is based on designs by Michelangelo. The equestrian statue in the middle of the square is an exact copy of a statue of Marcus Aurelius from the 2nd century. The original can be found at the **Musei Capitolini,** spread over two palaces on the square. These were the first museums in the world that opened their doors to the public in 1734. The Palazzo dei Conservatori houses remnants of the enormous statue of Constantine, together with the *Lupa Capitolina,* an Etruscan sculpture from 500 B.C. of the mythical she-wolf suckling twins, Romulus and Remus.

piazza del campidoglio 1, www.museicapitolini.org, t: 06608, open daily 9:30am-7:30pm, entrance €15, bus piazza venezia

㉞ When Rome became an empire and the city rapidly expanded, it didn't take long before the central square, the Foro Romano, became too small. Soon the **Fori Imperiali** (imperial forums) were built. Julius Caesar constructed the first forum in 54 B.C., and his adopted son followed 50 years later with the Forum of Augustus. At the end of Via dei Fori Imperiali lies the Temple of Peace. There wasn't much room left for Emperor Nerva, so his forum is squeezed in between Augustus' and the temple. By that time the valley between Quirinal Hill and Capitoline was full, but this did not stop Emperor Trajan from building the biggest imperial forum of all: It borders Trajan's Market and Column.

via dei fori imperiali, always open, free entrance, bus piazza venezia/metro cavour

㉟ The opening of the **Colosseum** in A.D. 80 was celebrated with games that lasted 100 days and 100 nights. There were all different kinds of tournaments, from gladiator fights to hunting parties and likely even sea battles. The architect of the Colosseum designed a system through which all 50,000 spectators could enter and leave the arena in just a few minutes. This system is still used today in modern sports facilities.

piazza del colosseo 1, www.archeoroma.beniculturali.it, t: 0639967700, open daily 8:30am until one hour before sunset, entrance €12 (combo-ticket with palatine hill and forum), metro colosseo

㊱ The Basilica of **San Clemente** is a three-tiered complex of buildings dedicated to Pope Clemens I. It's built on top of a clandestine church from the 1st century

that was located in a large residential house. A church honoring Saint Clemente was built here three centuries later. In the courtyard of the old block of houses, ruins have been found of a small Mithraic temple, erected by the worshippers of the Persian god Mithras. This temple was destroyed by the Normans in 1084, after which Pope Paschalis II commissioned the construction of a new basilica. The developments the Basilica of San Clemente underwent are a testament to the rise of the Roman Catholic Church.

via labicana 95, www.basilicasanclemente.com, t: 067740021, open daily 9am-12:30pm & 3:30pm-6pm (oct-mar), 3pm-6pm (apr-sep), free entrance, metro colosseo

FOOD & DRINK

(1) **Taverna Pretoriana** has plenty to offer foodies. You always get a *bruschetta* with tomato to start with, and the wait staff is extremely accommodating. The place has everything it needs to become your staple.

via palestro 46-48, t: 064450273, open sun-fri noon-3:30pm & 6pm-midnight, price pasta €6, bus/metro termini

(6) **Panella** has a large selection of sweet and savory baked goods from different regions, from Sicilian *arancine* (risotto balls) to Roman *fagottini* (pastry). Coffee is served with a dollop of *crema* (custard).

via merulana 54, www.panellaroma.com, t: 064872435, open mon-thu 8am-11pm, fri-sat 8am-midnight, sun 8:30am-4pm, price caffè crema €1, metro vittorio emanuele

(8) The products at **Urbana 47** all come from Lazio, the region surrounding Rome, from the often-organic seasonal produce to the wines and beers that accompany them. The interior is a hodgepodge of retro furniture and every item here is for sale, including wines, marmalades, and other regional delicacies.

via urbana 47, www.urbana47.it, t: 0647884006, open mon-fri 8:30am-midnight, sat-sun 9:30am-midnight, price lunch €15, metro cavour

(10) **La Boccaccia** serves pizzas, pastas, and rice salads for just a couple of euros. Order your food to go, or sit on one of the bar stools and enjoy it right there.

Either way, with a fresh slice of pizza in your hand, you could almost be mistaken for a real Roman!

via leonina 73, www.pizzerialaboccaccia.it, t: 3404551968, open daily 9am-midnight, price slice of pizza €2.50, metro cavour

⑫ "Free your taste buds," is the motto at **Fafiuché.** They want their customers to try and enjoy new things like it's your last night on earth. So, order a glass of wine during the *aperitivo* hour and fill up on the buffet. Later at night, this colorful wine bar transforms into a restaurant. Many of their gourmet food items and specialty drinks are also sold here.

via della madonna dei monti 28, www.fafiuche.it, t: 066990968, open mon-sat 5:30pm-1am, price aperitivo €8 (from 6:30pm), metro cavour

⑬ Rustic pizzeria **Alle Carrette** has indoor and outdoor seating. You can choose between a thin Roman pizza and a thick Neapolitan one. The fried *antipasti* are made fresh in the kitchen at this classic joint.

via della madonna dei monti 95, t: 066792770, open thu-mon noon-4pm & 7pm-11:30pm, tue-wed 7pm-11:30pm, price pizza €6, metro cavour

⑭ Family restaurant **La Taverna dei Fori Imperiali** takes pride in having served celebrity guests, including Dustin Hoffman and Al Pacino. They are equally happy to welcome mere mortals, making this a favorite haunt amongst Roman locals. Popular dishes include classic recipes, as well as surprising specialties like *gnocchi al tartufo*.

via della madonna dei monti 9, www.latavernadeiforiimperiali.com, t: 066798643, open mon & wed-sun 12:30pm-3pm & 7:30pm-10:30pm, price pasta €9, metro cavour

⑮ The interior at **Enoteca Cavour 313** is intimate, with wooden details and cozy private seating. You can buy wine every day from 12:30pm onwards, and it's a great place for tasting several varieties. The staff is very knowledgeable and they have an extensive wine selection. This *bistro all'italiano* also serves up a great dinner.

via cavour 313, www.cavour313.it, t: 066785496, open daily 12:30pm-2:45pm & mon-thu 6pm-11:30pm, fri-sat 6pm-midnight, sun 7pm-11pm, closed jul-aug, price glass of wine €4, metro cavour

㉖ Giacomo della Porta designed the fountain on Piazza Madonna dei Monti at the end of the 16th century. Young people sit here at night with plastic cups in hand—a local custom. There are multiple bars on the square, but we recommend **Civico 4** for a good glass of wine and authentic Italian food.

via degli zingari 4, www.civico4.it, t: 0648913460, open daily 5pm-midnight, price wine €5, metro cavour

㉗ Soft jazz and candlelight set the tone at **Al Vino Al Vino.** The wine menu is impressive, with many unique options that you can enjoy with some olives on the side. The menu is short, but for €1 you can enjoy a small plate with fresh zucchini, dried tomatoes, and homemade *caponata* (stewed eggplant). Open some mornings for wine sales.

via dei serpenti 19, t: 06485803, open mon-thu & sun 5:30pm-12:30am, fri-sat 5:30pm-1:30am, price glass of wine €5, metro cavour

㉘ **Pasta Imperiale** is owned by a young and vibrant couple, and they've opened a second location as well. The fresh pasta you choose from the tempting display

case is ready to eat within three minutes. The high tables and open kitchen make this a very pleasant place to stop for lunch.

via del boschetto 112, t: 324723203, open daily noon-5pm & 6:30pm-11:30pm, price pasta €4, metro cavour

㉔ **L'Asino d'Oro** is a "neo-*trattoria*"—a restaurant with a modern and sunny interior where you can delight in contemporary versions of Umbrian dishes and more, such as rabbit haunch or beef with cocoa. Chef Lucio Sforza's lunch menu is a very good deal.

via del boschetto 73, t: 0648913832, open tue-sat 12:30pm-11pm, price pasta €12, metro cavour

㉕ Romans have been quenching their thirst for wine at **Ai Tre Scalini** since 1895 and it is still just as popular today. Night after night young and old gather here together, and when it becomes too crowded, the party often spills out onto the street. Choose one of their great wines and order something regional to snack on, like *cicoria* or *porchetta*.

via panisperna 251, www.aitrescalini.org, t: 0648907495, open daily 12:30pm-1am, price glass of wine €5, metro cavour

㉘ The province of Rome promotes local products like ice cream, wine, and cookies with its own *Enoteca Provincia Romana*. For several years **Terre e Domus** was one of these so-called EPRs. The cool setting with a view of Trajan's Column and the Imperial Forums is breathtaking.

largo di foro traiano 82-84, t: 0669940273, open daily 9am-midnight, price glass of wine €5, bus/tram piazza venezia

㉝ **Caffè Capitolino** is part of the Musei Capitolini, but you can also have a coffee without visiting the museum. The self-service café inside has reasonable prices, but lunch on the terrace outside is definitely worth paying that little bit extra: The views of Rome are simply spectacular.

piazzale caffarelli 4, t: 0669190564, open tue-sun 9:30am-7pm, price sandwich €5.50, pizza €12, bus piazza venezia

SHOPPING

⑦ Treat yourself to an Italian makeover at **Smalto** with large sunglasses, flirty dresses, and high stiletto heels. Owners Giorgio and Pietro organize events on a regular basis, during which you can browse through the racks with a glass of wine in hand. Take this guide with you for proper VIP treatment!

via urbana 12, t: 064873645, open mon-sat 9:30am-8pm, metro cavour

⑪ Looking for a chocolate sculpture of the Colosseum or St. Peter? The delicious scent when you walk into **La Bottega del Cioccolato** will make it hard to decide. The chocolate monuments have recently become available in a practical "slice" version, as well. Don't forget to check out the rows of pralines while you're here.

via leonina 82, www.labottegadelcioccolato.it, t: 064821473, open mon-sat 9:30am-7:30pm (closed jul-aug), metro cavour

⑱ Looking at the many clothing shops in Monti, it's obvious that retro is back in style. Take **Pifebo Vintage Shop,** for example—it's a small, colorful boutique that sells all kinds of vintage fashion items, like jackets, T-shirts, and bags. This is the go-to shop to lend your look some retro and vintage flavor. They have their own line of sunglasses.

via dei serpenti 141, www.pifebo.com, t: 0689015204, open mon-sat 11am-3pm & 4pm-8pm, sun noon-8pm, metro cavour

㉑ In shop/studio **Le Nou** two young designers make the cutest little dresses, shirts, trousers, and jackets. Their shirts start at a mere €30—perfect if you're looking for exclusivity without breaking the bank.

via del boschetto 111, t: 0631056339, open mon-sat noon-8pm, oct-dec sun 3pm-8m, metro cavour

㉒ The furniture and accessories at **Estremi** come from all corners of the world: cashmere from Mongolia, embroidered fabrics from Uzbekistan, and candlesticks from Mexico. The owners of this shop are constantly traveling in search of special, yet affordable, merchandise.

via del boschetto 2a, www.estremiroma.com, t: 064744001, open mon-sat 10am-2pm & 4pm-8pm, metro cavour

㉓ Flowery prints and color blocks, dresses, and tunics—at **Kokoro** you're guaranteed to find the perfect piece. When a customer enters the store, needles and thread are temporarily put on hold. None of the items cost more than €70, yet everything is of very high quality. Customers leave this shop feeling *kokoro*—balanced in heart and soul.

via del boschetto 75, www.kokoroshop.it, t: 064870657, open daily 11am-8pm, metro cavour

MORE TO EXPLORE

⑲ Ready for a hair makeover? The stylists at **Contesta Rock Hair** are happy to help! They have salons in New York, Miami, and Shanghai and are up to speed on the latest hair trends. Customers receive a ten percent discount on Tuesday afternoons.

via degli zingari 9, www.contestarockhair.com, t: 0647823717, open tue & fri-sat 9am-7:30pm, wed-thu 10am-10pm, metro cavour

㉙ A visit to **Palazzo Valentini** is like stepping into a time machine: The *domus romane,* houses for rich Romans in Imperial times, come to life. Floors, mosaics, decorations, walls, kitchens, and bath houses are all highlighted in a stunning digital tour. Reservations are recommended.

via iv novembre 119a, www.palazzovalentini.it, t: 0632810, open wed-mon 9:30am-6:30pm, entrance €12, bus/tram piazza venezia

㉛ The gigantic, white, patriotic **Vittoriano** monument on Piazza Venezia was built for the first king of Italy, Vittorio Emanuele II. Many Italians see it as an eyesore and they mockingly call it "the wedding cake." Others consider this building an impressive architectural masterpiece. Inside, you can view the Altare della Patria (Altar of the Fatherland), which is guarded day and night. This is also where you'll find the Museo del Risorgimento, which covers the century before the unification. There is a restaurant on top of the Vittoriano with a spectacular view out over the city.

piazza venezia, t: 066780664, open 9:30am-4:30pm (winter), 9:30am-5:30pm (summer), free entrance, bus piazza venezia

WALK 6

ROMAN FORUM, AVENTINE HILL & TESTACCIO

ABOUT THE WALK

Depending on your interests, this walk can be more historic (Roman Forum) or contemporary and neighborhoody (Testaccio). Looking for some peace and quiet? Aventine Hill is the place to go. Start early in the morning, when the sun is not yet at its brightest, as the archaeological sites offer little shelter from its glare.

THE NEIGHBORHOODS

The center of ancient Rome is like an enormous open-air museum. Take your time to explore the **Roman Forum:** These ruins once stood at the heart of a vast empire. Ancient streets that have been here since time immemorial pass through the remnants of important temples. To this day the entire area remains a much-loved object of study for archaeologists.

Palatine Hill, where the remnants of two villages of the Iron Age were found, overlooks the 500-yard-long **Circus Maximus.** Today it is a bleak-looking wasteland, but with a little imagination you can picture chariots racing past like in the classic film *Ben Hur*, with 300,000 spectators cheering them on.

Climbing Aventine Hill on a hot and sunny day in Rome can be taxing, but the phenomenal view from the Orange Garden makes it all worthwhile. Be sure to peek through the mysterious Knights of Malta keyhole in the central *portone* (doorway) at **Piazza dei Cavalieri di Malta** for a perfect view of St. Peter's Basilica.

The working-class Testaccio neighborhood has yet to be discovered by tourists, but the vibe is great. Besides clubs and restaurants, this area holds several surprise attractions. Who would expect to find a pyramid in the middle of Rome or a hill constructed from Roman potsherds?

For the longest time Testaccio was dominated by a large slaughterhouse: the Mattatoio. Workers were often paid in part with cuts of meat nobody else wanted: offal, heads, and tails. To make this meat palatable, housewives had to be innovative and creative. This is where many typical Roman dishes stem from, such as *coda alla vaccinara* (braised oxtail) or *trippa alla romana* (tripe in tomato sauce with cheese and mint). Nowadays part of the slaughterhouse is a modern museum—a great example of how Rome has adapted to the times.

SHORT ON TIME? HERE ARE THE HIGHLIGHTS
+ PALATINO + ROMAN FORUM + PIAZZA DEI CAVALIERI DI MALTA
+ PYRAMID + MERCATO DI TESTACCIO

TIPS
// Essential archaeological excavations
// Not suitable on bike
// Testaccio is one of the least touristy areas of Rome

SIGHTS & ATTRACTIONS

① The **Arco di Costantino** was built in the year A.D. 315 in honor of Emperor Constantine, who liberated Rome from the tyrant Maxentius. The triumphal arch is ornately decorated, but only the smallest reliefs alongside the edges refer to Emperor Constantine. The rest relate to the reigns of other leaders, such as Trajan, Hadrian, and Marcus Aurelius.

between via di san gregorio and piazza del colosseo, metro colosseo

② Archaeological excavations on the **Palatino** (Palatine Hill) revealed the huts of Romulus—settlements that have been here since the beginning of the Iron Age. The elite lived on this hill during the Roman Republic, and gigantic palaces were built here during Imperial times. The Palatine museum displays remnants of frescoes, statues, bas-reliefs, and other objects found on the hill. And after many restorations, the Casa di Augusto (House of Augustus) is now also open to the public.

via di san gregorio 30, www.archeoroma.beniculturali.it, t: 0639967700, open daily 8:30am until one hour before sunset, entrance €12 (combo-ticket with colosseo and foro romano), metro colosseo

③ The **Foro Romano** (Roman marketplace) was the political, commercial, and religious center of the Republic of Rome. This is where the Senate met and politicians delivered their speeches. Merchants came here to do business, priests made offerings, and people shopped for goods and talked about the latest news. When the power of the Roman Empire declined, the Forum deteriorated. It took on a whole new role in the 5th century A.D. Farmers would bring their cattle to graze and the Forum was renamed Campo Vaccino (cow pasture). The stunning marble temples were looted. During the Middle Ages and Renaissance, architects sourced their building materials from here. Excavations of the ancient Forum began during the 19th century.

entrance largo della salara vecchia (on via dei fori imperiali)/entrance via di san gregorio 30, www.archeoroma.beniculturali.it, open daily 8:30am until one hour before sunset, entrance €12 (combo-ticket with colosseum and palatine hill), metro colosseo/bus/tram piazza venezia

④ The **Arco di Tito**—the triumphal Arch of Titus—was built in A.D. 81 in honor of Emperor Titus to mark his victory over Jerusalem. The reliefs on the inside of the arch depict the sacred inventory of the Jewish temple in Jerusalem. Other reliefs depict the triumphant homecoming, with Romans carrying their spoils from the temple. For a long time the arch stood as a symbol of the defeat of the Jews. Now it's considered one of the most beautiful ruins of the Forum.

see foro romano, metro colosseo/bus/tram piazza venezia

⑤ The construction of the last and largest Roman basilica, the **Basilica di Massenzio e Costantino,** began under Emperor Maxentius and was completed under Emperor Constantine in A.D. 312. Now the word "basilica" signifies a church, but in ancient times, it was no more than a covered hall and meeting place. The building was 330 feet long and 213 feet wide, and in the apse (the extension of the choir) stood an enormous statue of Constantine. Parts of this sculpture, including the 8.5-foot-tall head, are now on display at the Musei Capitolini.

see foro romano, metro colosseo/bus/tram piazza venezia

⑥ **Via Sacra** was the most important street in the center of ancient Rome. Its name stems from the many temples that lined this street. Generals who had won a war could request that the Senate hold a victory parade here. However, there were a few requirements: They needed to have conquered a significant amount of new territory and killed at least 5,000 enemy soldiers. During the parade, battles were re-enacted, POWs marched through the street, and spoils of war were put on display. Finally, the enemy leader was executed in public.

see foro romano, metro colosseo/bus/tram piazza venezia

⑦ Emperor Antoninus Pius commissioned the construction of the **Tempio di Antonino e Faustina** in honor of his late wife, Faustina. When he died, the temple was also dedicated to him. The Romans repurposed the temple into a church in the 8th century, using the antique columns as its entrance. After numerous excavations, the door of the temple now sticks out above street level and appears to be floating.

see foro romano, metro colosseo/bus/tram piazza venezia

⑧ Vesta, the goddess of the hearth, was very important in ancient Rome, as was the small, round **Tempio di Vesta.** Romans believed that Rome would fall if the fire in the temple ever went out. The six virgins who lived in the **Casa delle Vestali** (House of the Vestals) were in charge of keeping the fire burning. Young girls would enter the house between the ages of 6 and 10 and would stay here for a total of 30 years. During the first 10 years they would learn about fulfilling their duties, the following 10 involved keeping the fire burning, and throughout the final 10 they would pass on their knowledge. The house was a kind of monastery. The Vestal Virgins were highly respected and enjoyed certain privileges, but the rules were strict: If the holy fire ever went out or their chastity came into question, they were buried alive.

see foro romano, metro colosseo/bus/tram piazza venezia

⑨ When Julius Caesar was killed in 44 B.C., many Romans refused to believe he was really dead, so the Senate decided to hold his cremation in public. Caesar's adopted son, Augustus, deified him and commissioned the construction of the **Tempio del Divo Giulio**—the Temple of the Divine Julius.

see foro romano, metro colosseo/bus/tram piazza venezia

⑩ The **Curia** is where the Senate met. A group of 300 men would debate laws and subsequently advise the two consuls that ruled the Republic. The Curia was transformed into a church during the Middle Ages, but everything was reverted to its original design in the 1930s. The Curia stands exactly half as tall as the sum of its width and length, which, according to 1st-century architect Vitruvius, produces the best acoustics.

see foro romano, metro colosseo/bus/tram piazza venezia

⑪ The **Arco di Settimio Severo**—the triumphal Arch of Septimius Severus— was built in A.D. 203 to commemorate the 10th anniversary of Emperor Severus' victory over the Parthians (an Indo-Iranian people) and to honor his sons, Caracalla and Geta. A statue of Severus and his two sons in a chariot with six horses once stood here. Caracalla became emperor in A.D. 212 and killed his brother and co-emperor, Geta. Severus then had Geta's name removed everywhere *(damnatio memoriae)*.

see foro romano, metro colosseo/bus/tram piazza venezia

⑬ You will need to use your imagination when looking at the pile of sand that once was **Circo Massimo.** This is where the emperors of Rome organized chariot races that were often frequented by some 300,000 spectators. There were barely any rules to speak of, so accidents were commonplace. This has been a place for sports since the 6th century B.C., and to this day you will see joggers run their daily route here.

via del circo massimo, metro circo massimo

⑯ There are two temples left on the **Foro Boario** (the ancient cattle market). These date back to the 1st and 2nd centuries B.C. and have been so well maintained because they were used as churches in later years. The round temple was dedicated to Hercules Victor, and the square one—a typical Roman design with a covered entrance at the front—to Portunes, the god of ports and harbors. One of the most important ports of the Tiber River was close by.

piazza della bocca della verità, bus bocca della verità/metro circo massimo

⑰ Do not attempt to visit the **Bocca della Verità** unless you have a clear conscience. As Gegory Peck explained to Audrey Hepburn in *Roman Holiday,* rumor has it that the "Mouth of Truth" will bite the hand off a liar. According to local legend, a magician who wanted to test the virtue of married women cast a spell on this statue. Try it yourself, and then visit the neighboring church while you're there. The Santa Maria in Cosmedin church is famous for its 12th-century floors, frescoes, and the shards of mosaics in the sacristy.

piazza della bocca della verità, church open daily 10am-1pm & 3pm-5pm, free entrance, bus bocca della verità/metro circo massimo

㉓ Back when Egypt was still part of the Roman Empire—and Julius Caesar had his sights set on Cleopatra—Romans went wild over anything Egyptian. Nubian slaves, obelisks, and Egyptian gods were all the rage and the city was obsessed with this ancient culture. Nobleman Caio Cestio took it a step further and had a gigantic pyramid built on his grave (**Piramide di Caio Cestio**), measuring 100 Roman square feet (97 square feet today) at the base and standing 125 Roman feet (121 feet) high. You can visit the structure, but you have to make reservations.

piazzale ostiense, t: 0639967700, open 2nd and 4th saturday of the month at 11am, metro piramide

㉔ Over 4,000 non-Catholic foreigners who died in Rome after the end of the 18th century are buried at the beautiful **Cimitero Acattolico** cemetery. Some of the best known are poets, including John Keats, Percy Shelley, and Julius— Johann Wolfgang von Goethe's only son. The founder of the Italian communist party, Antonio Gramsci, is buried here as well.

via caio cestio 6, www.cemeteryrome.it, t: 065741900, open mon-sat 9am-5pm, sun & holidays 9am-1pm, free entrance, metro piramide

㉕ At first, **Monte Testaccio** looks like a perfectly normal green hill. But take a closer look and you'll see it's made of Roman potsherds, roof tiles, and other debris. This used to be the landfill for warehouses along the river. You can see cross-sections of the hill in many restaurants located around its base. Nowadays, the neighborhood around Monte Testaccio is known for its nightlife, and you can dance here until the wee hours.

via nicola zabaglia 24, t: 060608, open only by appointment, hill entrance €4, bus via marmorata/metro piramide

㉗ **MACRO Testaccio** museum is located in a former 19th-century slaughter-house, of which the steel construction is still very visible. This provides a unique and somewhat enigmatic contrast with the modern art on the walls. They have special exhibitions and organize events mostly geared toward a younger audience.

piazza orazio giustiniani 4, www.museomacro.org, t: 06671070400, open tue-sun 4pm-10pm, entrance €13.50, bus via marmorata/metro piramide

FOOD & DRINK

⑫ Chef Massimiliano Torres' trademark is simple dishes prepared with his signature style. The kitchen is at the heart of **Rosso,** and you can watch the cooks working their magic through the window in the red door. Choose from dishes such as Florentine-style steak, sautéed shrimps with olives and bread crumbs, or a variety of different burgers, including several vegetarian and vegan options.

viale aventino 32, www.rossoristora.it, t: 0664420656, open mon-fri 7am-1am, sat 8am-1am, sun 11am-1am, price soup €10, metro circo massimo

DINNER

TUTTI I GIORNI

19.00 - 01:00

RISTORANTE

APERITIVO

€ 8/10

TUTTI I GIORNI

18:30 - 21:00
(DOM 22:00)

BIRRA MORETTI

Dal 1859

⑭ **San Teo** is a French-style *pasticceria* where you can drink coffee at the bar with *mignons*—special single-bite versions of treats like tiramisu, cheesecake, or *Sachertorte*. You can also get these miniature pastries to go.

via di san teodoro 88, t: 0669920945, open daily 7am-8pm, price mignon €0.70, metro circo massimo/bus teatro di marcello

㉖ Alfredo runs the classic restaurant **Pecorino** (named after the Italian sheep-milk cheese) together with his wife and daughters. Enjoy typical Roman dishes with fresh ingredients from the market, such as *fettuccine alla gricia* and the *semifreddo allo zabaione* for dessert.

via galvani 64, www.ristorantepecorino.it, t: 0657250539, open tue-sun 12:30pm-2:30pm & 8pm-11pm, price pasta €12, bus via marmorata/metro piramide

㉙ Vegetarians should probably skip **Agustarello,** because almost every dish here is made with meat—mostly *quinto quarto* (organ meats). This simple restaurant in Testaccio has been around for years and is as Roman as it gets.

via giovanni branca 98, t: 065746585, open mon-sat 12:30pm-3pm & 7:30pm-11:30pm, price pasta €10, bus via marmorata

㉛ The chef at **Felice a Testaccio** serves a different traditional dish every day, such as *tortellini* on Mondays and fish on Fridays. The menu features daily specials, but mainstays such as *involtini in sugo* (beef rolls) are popular favorites at this busy restaurant.

via mastro giorgio 29, www.feliceatestaccio.it, open mon-sat 12:30pm-3pm & 7:30pm-11:15pm, price pasta €10, bus via marmorata/metro piramide

㉞ Halogen lights and a long line of people typify **Pizzeria Nuovo Mondo.** This is how Romans like to eat their pizza—without any fuss and in a large, noisy space. The pizzas are delicious, as are the *antipasti* such as *bruschetta al ciauscolo* (with sausage).

via amerigo vespucci 15, t: 065746004, open tue-sun 6:30pm-12:30am, price pizza €6, bus via marmorata/metro piramide

㉟ Restaurant Emporio Club, or **Rec23** for short, is the place to go in Testaccio for a cocktail or an *aperitivo*. Their buffet is plentiful and you can keep filling up your plate until 9pm. This beautiful restaurant is great for dinner. We highly recommend it for a night out in an authentic Roman setting.

piazza dell'emporio 1-2, www.rec23.com, t: 0687462147, open daily 6:30pm-2am, price aperitif €8, bus via marmorata/metro piramide

SHOPPING

㉑ Owner Alessio Gigliani's personal sense of style tells you all you need to know about **Dandy's:** This is the go-to shop for that famous Italian elegance. Order a custom-made shirt (if you have time—it will take 15 days), or choose one of the many beautiful ready-made shirts for sale. They also sell their own line of high-quality, hand-stitched ties.

via galvani 5, www.dandys.it, t: 065750696, open mon 4pm-8pm, tue-sat 9:30am-1:30pm & 4pm-8pm, bus via marmorata/metro piramide

㉒ The two **Volpetti** brothers have been running their shop of Italian delicacies since 1973. The huge range of products is a sight to see. They have a *tavola calda* on the side street just around the corner, where you can sit down for a plate of pasta.

via marmorata 47, www.volpetti.com, t: 065742352, open mon-sat 8am-2pm & 5pm-8:15pm, bus via marmorata/metro piramide

㉚ **Ctonia** is special without being pretentious. In this tiny boutique you'll find a unique range of contemporary women's wear and shoes. You'll find no high heels or evening gowns, but rather original, everyday fashion.

via aldo manuzio 48, t: 065743266, open mon-sat 10am-1:30pm & 4pm-8pm, bus via marmorata/metro piramide

㉜ Owner Irene found out by accident that the name of her shop, **Kast** (Dutch for "closet"), was very appropriate for a clothing store. She sells women's fashion and accessories from the most prestigious brands.

piazza testaccio 33, www.abbigliamentodonnakast.com, t: 065759368, open mon-sat 10am-1:30pm & 3:30pm-7:30pm, bus via marmorata/metro piramide

㉝ What could be a better souvenir than a new pair of Italian shoes? **Moretti** sells beautiful footwear you'll want to take home.

via g.b. bodoni 5 b/c, t: 065746998, open mon-sat 9am-1pm & 4pm-8pm (winter 15:30pm-7:30pm), bus via marmorata/metro piramide

MORE TO EXPLORE

⑮ Every weekend, local artisans and farmers flock to the city to sell their wares in market halls like **Mercato di Campagna Amica.** Here you can see, sample, and shop for fresh fruits and vegetables, wines and oils, dairy products, fish, sausages, hams, bread, and flowers. Almost all the produce and foods are from heirloom varieties and everything is produced without genetic modification.

via di san teodoro 74, www.mercatocircomassimo.it, t: 06489931, open sep-jun sat 9am-6pm, sun 9am-4pm, jul sat 9am-6pm, closed aug, bus bocca della verità/metro circo massimo

⑱ Visit the rose gardens **Roseto Comunale** in May and June for a lovely walk when the flowers are in bloom and the gardens are open to the public. In June the smaller competition garden is open, too. A Jewish cemetery was once located where the gardens are now. The paths and plantings (when viewed from above) are shaped like a Menorah, the seven-branched candelabrum, commemorating the former cemetery.

via di valle murcia 6, t: 065746810, open daily mid apr-mid jun 8:30am-7:30pm, free entrance, metro circo massimo

⑲ The **Giardino degli Aranci** was built within the medieval walls of an ancient fortress on Aventine Hill belonging to the Savelli family. It's one of the prettiest places in town. You have a magnificent view of the city center below from amongst the garden's orange trees.

piazza pietro d'illiria, open daily sunrise to sunset, free entrance, metro circo massimo

⑳ On **Piazza dei Cavalieri di Malta,** you can enjoy a rather unique view: Peer through the keyhole in the wall of the monastery church for a fantastic view of St. Peter's Basilica. You may have to stand in line, but it is well worth the wait. This monastery church used to belong to the knights of the Order of Malta, known for their crusades. Now it represents their own sovereign state, complete with head of state, passports, and license plates.

piazza dei cavalieri di malta 4, www.orderofmalta.org, metro circo massimo

㉘ A few years ago the **Mercato di Testaccio** was relocated, creating a totally new image as a result. The market stalls are housed in white "boxes," selling everything from fruits and veg to meats, pastries, flowers, and even clothing. Take your time to stroll past the different vendors and feel the vibe of this neighborhood.

via beniamino franklin, open mon-sat 6am-3pm, bus via marmorata/metro piramide

WITH MORE TIME

The walks in this book will take you to most of the city's main highlights. Of course, there are still a number of sights worth seeing that are not included in these walks. These are listed below. Note that not all of these places are easily accessible by foot from town, but you can get to them all using public transportation.

Ⓐ **San Giovanni in Laterano** is Rome's cathedral and the seat of the Pope (as bishop of the city). The church was founded in the 4th century and has slowly but steadily expanded since then. Only the pope is allowed to deliver the service from the high altar. The cathedral has a beautiful cloister, too. On the north end of the square, in front of the cathedral, are the Holy Steps, or **Scala Santa.** According to legend, Christ walked on these before his crucifixion. Pilgrims ascend the stairs on their knees, praying for mercy.

piazza di san giovanni in laterano, www.vatican.va, t: 0669886433, cathedral open daily 7am-6:30pm, monastery 9am-6pm, scala santa 6am-1pm & 3pm-6:30pm, monastery, cathedral, and scala santa entrance €2, metro san giovanni

Ⓑ It always takes forever for something new to be built in Rome. A mere 15 years passed before **Maxxi** was finally able to open its doors. This museum, with art from the 21st century, was designed by female architect Zaha Hadid. Together with the auditorium designed by Renzo Piano and the pedestrian bridge designed by Buro Happold, it's a pinnacle of modern architecture in this ancient city.

via guido reni 4a, www.fondazionemaxxi.it, t: 63201954, open tue-fri & sun 11am-7pm, sat 11am-10pm, entrance €10, metro flaminio, then tram apollodoro

Ⓒ **EUR** is short for "Esposizione Universale di Roma." This neighborhood was commissioned by Mussolini for a World's Fair that never happened. Construction started in the late 1930s. The gigantic, angular white buildings in fascist style have a strange yet intriguing appearance. The Palazzo della Civiltà Italiana is especially interesting. Visit the website for information on the various museums in EUR.

metro eur palasport/eur fermi, www.romaeur.it

Ⓓ **Via Appia Antica** was one of the most important streets in ancient Rome. You can still see palaces from ancient times, the first Christian catacombs, and the graves of Roman nobility. It's very bikeable—you can rent bikes at the information center at the start of the street. Motorized traffic is not allowed on Sundays and holidays, apart from city buses (lines #118 and #218) and the Archeobus shuttle bus. With your ticket (€15), you can hop on and off to see the old street and the park around it.

via appia antica begins at porta san sebastiano, practical information: www. parcoappiaantica.it, www.trambusopen.com, t: 065126314

Ⓔ **Ostia Antica** is at least as interesting as Pompeii, but without the hordes of tourists. Ostia was once a port town, but fell into disrepair in the 7th century when trade went downhill and its inhabitants began dying of malaria. The city has been well preserved, including the forum, temples, and amphitheater.

ostia antica, entrance via dei romagnoli 717, www.ostia-antica.org, t: 656358099, open tue-sun 8:30am-7:30pm (ticket counter closes at 6pm), price €6.50, train roma-lido, leaves from metro piramide

Ⓕ The **Terme di Caracalla** are some of the most impressive ruins from ancient Rome. The complex did not solely consist of baths—it was a proper spa resort with fitness rooms, sports fields, a library, dance halls, steam rooms, massage spaces, and swimming pools. The baths were open to all Romans and held up to 1,600 people at a time.

via delle terme di caracalla 52, www.archeoroma.beniculturali.it, t: 0639967700, open daily 9am until one hour before sunset, entrance €6, metro circo massimo

Ⓖ During renovation works in the Capitoline Museums in 1997, hundreds of statues had to be moved to another location because there wasn't enough room onsite. This resulted in the **Centrale Montemartini,** a museum of antiquity housed in the oldest power plant in Rome. The exhibition was supposed to be temporary, but was so successful it became permanent. You can see funeral objects and many sculptures from the Roman Republic. Keep your eye on the website for special concerts and tasting parties that take place on a regular basis.

via ostiense 106, www.centralemontemartini.org, open tue-sun 9am-7pm, entrance €7.50, metro piramide/bus 23

Ⓗ The **Parco degli Acquedotti** became well known to the public thanks to a scene from the movie *La Grande Bellezza.* It's a nearly 600-acre park with two gigantic ancient Roman aqueducts and several archaeological finds from different eras. Come here for a nice, relaxing walk and to learn more about the craftsmanship of the Romans—all in a natural setting.

via lemonia 256, www.parcoacquedotti.it, t: 65135316, always open, free entrance, metro lucio sesto/giulio agricola/subaugusta

Ⓘ The Sunday **Porta Portese** flea market is a must for bargain hunters: almost 1.4 miles with nothing but clothing, antiques, and household items. The market has been an institution in Rome for decades.

from piazza di porta portese, through via portuense, open sun 6am-2pm, bus/tram viale di trastevere

Ⓙ Many a classic movie was shot in the **Cinecittà** film studios, including *Ben Hur* and *We Have a Pope,* but more surprisingly, *The English Patient* and *Gangs of New York.* Take the English tour, walk through the sets and imagine you're wandering around 15th-century Florence or the America of three centuries ago. The museum showcases costumes from movie royalty like Elizabeth Taylor and Clint Eastwood.

via tuscolana 1055, www.cinecittasimostra.it, t: 688816182, open wed-mon 9:30am-6:30pm, entrance exhibition and tour €20, metro cinecittà

(K) Take the direct train from Trastevere and in 40 minutes you'll be in Anguillara. From here it's only a short taxi ride to get to **Lago di Bracciano** (Lake Bracciano), the ideal place for a relaxing day on the water. Romans love to leave their busy city behind and cool down at this lake in the crater of a dormant volcano.

lago di bracciano (30 mi north west of rome), www.turismobracciano.com, train anguillara and taxi (approx. 4 mi)

(L) In the year 312, pagan Emperor Constantine had a vision at **Ponte Milvio.** A cross appeared to him with the text *In hoc signo vinces:* "In this sign you will conquer." After that, he defeated his opponent Maxentius and became more open to Christianity. The first restoration work started on the bridge in the 15th century. Both sides, the buildings, and the entry archway designed by Giuseppe Valadier are the result of innovations from 1805 under Pope Pius VII. Nowadays the neighborhood around the bridge is the party center of north Rome and is brimming with clubs, bars, and restaurants. It's also worth visiting during the day, especially for soccer fans: Stadio Olimpico sports stadium is a stone's throw away.

ponte milvio, tram 2/bus 280

AFTER DARK

Rome is not known for its nightlife. For big clubs frequented mostly by locals, you'll have to leave the center. Via di Monte Testaccio—the so-called "nightclub street"—is an option in the city center.

There are, however, plenty of cafés and cocktail bars, especially in the Monti and Trastevere neighborhoods and around Piazza Navona and Campo de' Fiori. The San Lorenzo neighborhood, just east of Termini, is also worth a visit. It has a

studenty atmosphere. There are numerous surprising bars on Via del Pigneto, and the subway takes you there in no time.

Theaters and cinemas are not very international. Sometimes you can see movies in their original language in Cinema dei Piccoli and Multisala Barberini. If you want to see a concert or opera, head to the Auditorium or the Teatro dell'Opera.

We have all the latest up-to-date information about nightlife in Rome on our website—from swanky cocktail bars and popular wine bars to local pubs and popular clubs. Check out **www.timetomomo.com** and plan your own perfect night out in Rome.

HOTELS

A comfortable bed, a tasty breakfast, and a nice interior—these are all the essential ingredients for a pleasant hotel stay. Even more important, however, is location. A hotel is only really good if you can walk out of the lobby and straight into the bustling city.

Accommodations in Rome vary from tiny B&Bs to luxury hotels. Book early to get a better deal. Monti, Trastevere, and the historic center are very welcoming and quaint. Prati and Testaccio are quieter and great if you want to see the less-touristy, authentic Rome.

Prices around Termini Central Station are somewhat lower, but this is not where you will find the best accommodations. An address close to a subway stop is convenient if you want to see many sights. Before you book farther away from the center, check that the neighborhood is comfortable and safe.

WWW.TIMETOMOMO.COM

OUR PERSONAL SELECTION OF HOTELS IN
THE HOTTEST NEIGHBORHOODS IN TOWN.
GO ONLINE & CLICK TO BOOK.

INDEX

✳ INDEX

MOON ROME WALKS

FIRST EDITION

Avalon Travel
An imprint of Perseus Books
A Hachette Book Group company
1700 Fourth Street
Berkeley, CA 94710, USA
www.moon.com

ISBN 978-1-63121-604-6

Concept & Original Publication "time to momo Rome" © 2017 by mo'media.
All rights reserved.
For the latest on time to momo walks and recommendations, visit www.timetomomo.com.

MO'MEDIA

TEXT & WALKS
Tessa D.M. Vrijmoed

TRANSLATION
Cindi Sheridan-Heller

MAPS
Van Oort redactie & kartografie

PHOTOGRAPHY
Marjolein den Hartog, Fiona Ruhe, Vincent van den
Hoogen, Francesca Pirzio Biroli, Renate Reitler

DESIGN
Studio 100% & Oranje Vormgevers

PROJECT EDITORS
Heleen Ferdinandusse, Bambi Bogert

AVALON TRAVEL

PROJECT EDITOR:
Sierra Machado

COPY EDITOR:
Maggie Ryan

PROOFREADER:
Patty Mon

COVER DESIGN:
Derek Thornton, Faceout Studios

Printed in China by RR Donnelley
First U.S. printing, September 2017.

time to momo
MAP APP

Download your free time to momo app from www.timetomomo.com/apps, and know your way around town. For more information, go to:

www.timetomomo.com/mapapp

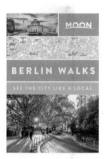

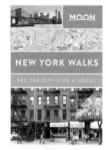
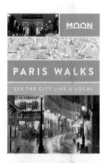